Troy Maxwell knows that the [illegible] Spirit may be one of the most misunderstood aspects of following Jesus—which is why *Under the Influence* is so relevant. Bringing insight and fresh application from the truth of God's Word, Troy reveals how we can experience God's power and presence in our daily lives by relying on His Spirit within us. This great resource will bless so many people as they befriend the Holy Spirit and grow closer to God.

—Chris Hodges
Senior Pastor, Church of the Highlands;
Author, *Out of the Cave* and *Pray First*

Under the Influence is more than a cute title; it's a daily reality in the life of a Christian believer. My father was a Pentecostal church pioneer in India. I was so blessed to be born in that home. I know firsthand the power of the Holy Spirit as well as when I'm trying to accomplish God assignments in my own strength. This book by my friend Troy Maxwell will challenge and inspire you and all those who serve the kingdom with you.

—Sam Chand
President Emeritus, Beulah Heights University

What an amazing resource to help believers understand the vital role of the Holy Spirit in our lives! This book is a must-read for all who long to see God move powerfully today!

—David and Jason Benham
Best-Selling Authors; Entrepreneurs

Under the Influence is a desperately needed message for the church today!

—Nathan Finochio
Founder and Director, TheosU

Troy Maxwell has done a masterful job demystifying one of the most mystical aspects of God Himself, the third person of the Trinity! The church at large will be enriched as they dive into this page-turning basic tutorial of understanding the implementation of the role of the Holy Spirit. The individual as well as corporate benefit will be undeniably clear before the end of chapter 1! This is one of those "I enjoy it, and it's good for me" kind of books. Troy has really outdone himself here. Read this book! You'll be exceedingly glad you did.

—Roger Archer
Pastor, Motion Church

Compelling and inspiring, Troy reminds us of the secret sauce for Christ followers. At a time in history when Christian culture is rapidly eroding and the need for authentic representations of Jesus is imperative, this book makes it clear that outside a relationship with the person of the Holy Spirit, it will not happen.

—Jay Stewart
Author; Founding and Lead Pastor,
The Refuge Church

Troy Maxwell tackles one of the greatest issues in the church today: What is the ministry of the Holy Spirit, and how are people to respond to it? In the New Testament there are two promises that transcend all others. There is the promise of Jesus, spoken of in John 3:16, securing heaven for each of us who believe in Him and giving us a future. But God also gives us the promise of the Holy Spirit, whom Jesus introduces in John 14:16–17. This second promise gives us power to live today. God wants us to have a future, which we find in Jesus, but He also wants us to have the divine enabling of the Holy Spirit to live for today. Life is too complicated and demanding; we need the Holy Spirit, who is greater than us and whose abilities exceed ours. Too often this promise is ignored, leaving Christians to navigate life with their own resources. This book is a great read, but more than that, it tells you how to have a great life.

—Gerald Brooks, DD, DCL

Under the Influence is a powerful resource for anyone who has questions about the Holy Spirit. It is a brilliant read for any and every believer.

—Marcus Mecum
Senior and Founding Pastor,
Seven Hills Church

UNDER THE INFLUENCE

UNDER THE INFLUENCE

TROY MAXWELL

For more resources like this visit the author's website at troymaxwell.com.

Cataloging-in-Publication Data is on file with the Library of Congress.

ISN: 978-1-960678-66-9 1 2 3 4 5 6 7 8 9

Printed in the United States of America

DEDICATION

I dedicate this book first to my Lord and Savior, Jesus. I am blown away by His grace and mercy in my life. I am so grateful that I get to do what I get to do. Every day is an adventure. The people I have met, the places I have been to, and the experiences I have experienced are sometimes overwhelming. Second, I dedicate this book to my loving and caring wife, Penny. She has stuck by my side for over thirty years. We have been through many ups and downs. We have traveled, raised three kids, and built an amazing church together. There is absolutely no way I would be the man I am today without the woman God gave me. I never could have dreamed we would get to do life as we do. I also want to thank my church, Freedom House, after more than twenty years of pastoring in the greatest city in the United States, Charlotte, North Carolina. I often send letters to people, and from early on I have signed them, "I love being your pastor." It is just as true today as it was when I started. Pastoring is not an easy thing, but the people make it worth it. Freedom House, I dedicate this book to you.

CONTENTS

INTRODUCTION

A GROUP OF AFRICAN tribal leaders traveled to Europe at the end of World War I to gain an understanding of the modern world and learn how to improve the leaders' communities. A general took them on a tour of England and Europe to see how cities functioned. The many sights, technologies, and new industries awed and inspired them. After several weeks they were treated to something special. The group spent its last night in Europe in a brand-new hotel in Paris that boasted indoor plumbing. Of everything these tribal leaders had seen, the hotel impressed them most—specifically the water faucets. For several hours they repeatedly turned on the faucets in awe of how the water would come on command. They kept turning the water on and off. These men lived in arid parts of the world where finding clean water sources took a great deal of energy and time. Tribes had to move from oasis to oasis, but here in this Paris hotel were devices that produced water on demand with the turn of a handle.

When the general went to pick up the African leaders, police had surrounded the Paris hotel. With fascination the tribal leaders had ripped all the faucets out of the hotel walls. They thought they could take them home and get the same results. They didn't realize the faucets were simply a tool to connect with the water source. The pipes that had the faucets attached were connected to a basement water source that supplied water to the entire hotel. The source was the important part.

When I see how some Christians live, I think of those tribal leaders trying to produce water from faucets connected to nothing. It is a picture of the Christian life without the influence of and baptism with the Holy Spirit. We may have the tools—the "faucets"—but we lack the connection to a "water" source. I believe every Christian—and every person—hungers to experience the full power and all the benefits of the gospel. They want to connect to the endless reservoir of the Holy Spirit's power, guidance, peace, and so much more. They want the lifestyle God designed for each believer to have, and they genuinely desire every reward Jesus bought with His death and resurrection.

But many Christians haven't walked in vibrant

fellowship with the Holy Spirit. They haven't related to the Holy Spirit the way He wants to relate to them, or experienced all the power and guidance He provides. People often close the door to His activity in their walk of faith. Some seem to define the Holy Spirit out of existence and have never involved Him after their salvation experience.

Many Christians and non-Christians consider the Holy Spirit mysterious and a little scary. Many faithful believers look to the Bible, Christian teachings, worship, and spending time with others to meet all their spiritual needs. They conclude that the Holy Spirit is somehow present in these things (which He is) but that there is nothing more to a relationship with Him. They view His active presence in their lives as unnecessary, superfluous—something not required to get by and that may even lead us astray.

It's as if the Holy Spirit is off to the side, waiting for us to invite Him in. And we're turning the handles on faucets we tore out of a hotel wall.

This is not how things were meant to be. Jesus talked a lot about the Holy Spirit before ascending into heaven. He called him "the Helper" (John 14:26) and said He would empower us in ways nobody on earth had ever known. Jesus' death and resurrection opened the door to a life with God. But Jesus Himself said the Christian life can be lived in partnership with the Holy Spirit—whom Jesus sent to be with us and in us at all times.

It may shock you, but when Jesus said He was going away and sending a helper, He was thinking of you and me. We all need a helper. The Holy Spirit is our necessary partner in life, the only One capable of giving daily peace, power, and critical guidance. Only He—the Holy Spirit, our daily companion—can provide these for our lives.

Maybe you haven't heard that a helper is available and ready to help you. Perhaps you have heard about the Holy Spirit's work but haven't leaned in to learn more. Maybe you got burned by bad teaching or weird practices (as many of us did at some point; see chapter 3). I meet gun-shy Christians all the time. I also meet those who get annoyed when the subject of the Holy Spirit comes up because they lack full understanding. They sense that they need a more vibrant and deeper relationship with Him, but they don't know how to get it.

The good news is that the Bible gives clear answers. What the Bible teaches about the Holy Spirit may surprise us at times, but there is nothing unclear about it. In fact, people mostly have the same questions about how to relate to our helper. I often get asked:

- Who is the Holy Spirit, and what is He like?
- What does He do for us?
- How can I know Him as my helper and companion?
- What does the Bible mean by being baptized in the Holy Spirit?

- How can I interact with the helper without becoming weird or getting into error?
- What is speaking in tongues, and is it for me?

These are just a few great questions about the Holy Spirit that this book will straightforwardly answer while shedding light on how a relationship with the helper works. You will gain greater clarity, enjoyment, and empowerment in your relationship with the Holy Spirit. You will learn to walk and talk with Him, access His help, and perceive His guidance.

Even for those who have walked with the Lord for many years, there is more. Each one of us can experience the Holy Spirit increasingly day by day—walking in the greater power, wisdom, and peace that Jesus planned for us to walk in. It is all by the work of this helper.

Whether you're learning about Him for the first time or seeking a refreshing of His power and presence in your life, I invite you to join me on this journey to explore who the Holy Spirit is, what He does, and how we can fully experience Him. Your walk with God will never be the same. I will have prayers throughout the book. I encourage you to take a moment to read them out loud and just wait a moment before you move on, to let God prepare your heart. I am believing this book will change your life. Pray this:

Heavenly Father, I ask that my heart and mind be open to hearing Your voice when it comes to my relationship with the third person of the Trinity, the Holy Spirit. I ask You to help me see Your plan for my life and how the Holy Spirit wants to be part of that plan. If Jesus said I need Him, then I expect an encounter with Him as I read this book and spend time with You. Please help me understand more fully! Help me grow closer to You! In Jesus' name, amen.

CHAPTER 1

UNDER THE INFLUENCE

OK, YOU MAY have noticed when you picked up this book that the cover looks like a label from a famous alcohol distributor. Now let me tell you why; please stick with me here.

When we talk about the influence of the Holy Spirit on our lives, we must look at the first time we see His influence at work *after* Jesus was raised from the dead. In Acts 2 the disciples prayed in Jerusalem as Jesus instructed. They were waiting for this promise He had told them was coming (Acts 1:4). They didn't necessarily know what was going on or what was going to happen. As it turned out, they were about to experience something powerful, supernatural, and maybe a little crazy.

Let's set the scene. The whole city overflowed with people who had come to celebrate the Passover. The disciples of Jesus were in this house in the city, on the top floor. The Bible tells us that the Holy Spirit—this promised One Jesus told them about—came and shook the house, filling each waiting disciple. Then they all started to pray and speak in languages they didn't know. (We will zoom in on this aspect later.) When the crowd saw this, they "were all amazed and perplexed, saying to one another, 'Whatever could this mean?' Others mocking said, 'They are full of new wine'" (Acts 2:12–13).

They knew something had happened, but they couldn't explain it. Then Peter stood up and delivered an incredible message to everyone in earshot. He started by saying: "For these are not drunk, as you suppose, since it is only the third hour of the day" (v. 15).

He told them, "It's only 9 a.m.!" (This time of day was called "the third hour" in those days.) Yet many in the crowd of thousands thought they were *under the influence* of alcohol—stumbling around drunk just after breakfast.

Pause a moment: This is one reason I love the Bible so much—it's so honest about how people behave. God was moving powerfully in these men and women, and many bystanders thought they were drunk. I don't know about you, but I laugh out loud when reading this. These disciples were under the influence, for sure, but it was the influence of the power of God, not alcohol. It was the Holy Spirit.

Allow me a moment of confession here. I have been drunk. It's been a very long time, and I was not a Christian then. I call it my BC days, "before Christ." But I can guarantee that back then, when I did drink, I didn't speak in another language about the wonderful works of God. I didn't say much at all, to be honest. See, the people watching were trying to explain something supernatural with a natural perspective. They saw a powerful influence on these people and did not know what it was.

Many influences are visible and external. We influence people with our words and actions or sometimes just by being in the same room with them. All this influence is from the outside. But when we receive the baptism of the Holy Spirit as these disciples did in the first two chapters of Acts, God influences us from the inside. He leads us from our hearts, minds, and souls.

When you become a Christian, you open yourself to a life far beyond what you see, hear, feel, and touch. You are now a candidate to live a supernatural life—a life led by God through the influence of the Holy Spirit.

A Hollywood Example

Let me build a bridge here. I am a movie guy; I love movies. I love going to the movie theater, the popcorn smell, and the sticky floor when you walk. These days they have super-comfortable reclining chairs. What's not to love?

I remember going to the theater to see a movie called *Limitless* in the early 2000s. Bradley Cooper played a guy struggling in life. Every corner of his existence was in shambles, and he couldn't get it together. Then one day, he had lunch with a family member, who gave him a new drug that hadn't hit the market yet—a pill supposed to unlock the unused parts of your brain.

Cooper's character didn't take the pill right away and didn't fully believe it could do what his family member said it could. But then, on the way up the stairs to his apartment, he popped it in and swallowed it. What happened was amazing.

On the screen everything visible to you, the moviegoer, began to clear up. Light started to appear, colors became crisper, things snapped into focus, and sounds became less muffled. What was so impactful about this was that until that moment, you hadn't noticed all the dulled-out details. But under the influence of the super pill, the character's world opened up.

In my view, Hollywood did a great job of showing what it feels and looks like when we are baptized in the Holy Spirit and then live our lives under His influence. Let me give two reasons, among so many, that having the Holy Spirit's full influence in your life matters.

Our Helper-God

One of the best reasons we should want and welcome the baptism of the Holy Spirit is simply that God wants to help us. This has always been His heart and plan for us, and the Holy Spirit carries it out on earth. We see hints and foreshadowing of the Holy Spirit's reality throughout the Bible.

One of my favorites is the story of a great military general with leprosy. Many people forget this story, but when you look at it, you can see the work of the Holy Spirit depicted in the actions of some humble people surrounding this mighty man. The story starts like this:

> Now Naaman, commander of the army of the king of Syria, was a great and honorable man in the eyes of his master, because by him the LORD had given victory to Syria. He was also a mighty man of valor, but a leper. And the Syrians had gone out on raids, and had brought back captive a young girl from the land of Israel. She waited on Naaman's wife. Then she said to her mistress, "If only my master were with the prophet who is in Samaria! For he would heal him of his leprosy." And Naaman went in and told his master, saying, "Thus and thus said the girl who is from the land of Israel."
>
> —2 KINGS 5:1–4

What I love about this story is that the helpful advice comes from key people who are never named. The girl giving good counsel is identified only as a young girl. As the story unfolds, more nameless servants step in to play critical roles in this afflicted military leader's decision-making:

> Then the king of Syria said, "Go now, and I will send a letter to the king of Israel."...
>
> Then Naaman went with his horses and chariot, and he stood at the door of Elisha's house. And Elisha sent a messenger to him, saying, "Go and wash in the Jordan seven times, and your flesh shall be restored to you, and you shall be clean." But Naaman became furious, and went away and said, "Indeed, I said to myself, 'He will surely come out to me, and stand and call on the name of the LORD his God, and wave his hand over the place, and heal the leprosy.' Are not the Abanah and the Pharpar, the rivers of Damascus, better than all the waters of Israel? Could I not wash in them and be clean?" So he turned and went away in a rage. And his servants came near and spoke to him, and said, "My father, if the prophet had told you to do something great, would you not have done it? How much more then, when he says to you, 'Wash, and be clean'?" So he went down and dipped seven times in the Jordan, according to the saying of the man of God; and his flesh was restored like the flesh of a little child, and he was clean.
>
> —2 KINGS 5:5, 9–14

When I read this, what jumps off the page is how clearly the servants and the young girl are a type of the Holy Spirit. What I mean by a "type" is that often the Old Testament foreshadows what is to come in the New Testament. Naaman was a picture of us dealing with a life-threatening situation, and these servants were helping him make the right decision, just as the Holy Spirit helps us. They acted the way the Holy Spirit acts and did the things He does, pointing us in the direction of God and influencing us. As a result, Naaman was encouraged to go to the River Jordan, wash seven times, and receive complete healing. A miracle followed this simple obedience.

You may think I'm stretching it, but once you see the pattern, it becomes evident that God foreshadowed the work of His Holy Spirit in many situations in the Old Testament. Whenever you find nameless servants seeking no credit but doing much to advise, guide, and comfort people in times of decision—that's a picture of the Holy Spirit. Their behavior perfectly portrays how the Holy Spirit helps those who choose to walk in the Spirit, always pointing us to God as our Healer, Deliverer, and Father.

Let's Emulate the Prototype

Here's another reason—and probably more important—for wanting everything the Holy Spirit has to give us. As Christians, we acknowledge and proclaim Jesus as our example; another way to put it is that He is our prototype, which means we are to be patterned after Him. He was full of the Holy Spirit. We should be full of the Holy Spirit too. Jesus came not to live for Himself but to make a way for us to do what He did and serve God and others the way He did.

As we investigate the relationship between Jesus and the Holy Spirit, we see that Jesus was the first to have the Spirit permanently living within Him. Before Jesus, the Holy Spirit came upon people for a purpose and a limited amount of time. He came upon Elijah (1 Kings 18:46), Samson (Judg. 14:6), Gideon (Judg. 6:34), and others, and they fulfilled their specific God assignments. Then the Holy Spirit lifted from them, only to return and rest upon them when they needed to fulfill another assignment or mission. This happened regularly.

Things radically changed beginning with Jesus' life. For the first time, the Holy Spirit permanently remained on a person. John the Baptist got the heads-up from God the Father about what was about to happen:

> The next day John saw Jesus coming toward him, and said, "Behold! The Lamb of God who takes away the sin of the world! This is He of whom I said, 'After me comes a Man who is preferred before me, for He was before me.' I did not know Him; but that He should be revealed to Israel, therefore I came baptizing with water."
>
> And John bore witness, saying, "I saw the Spirit descending from heaven like a dove, and He remained upon Him. I did not know Him, but He who sent me to baptize with water said to me,

> 'Upon whom you see the Spirit descending, and *remaining on Him*, this is He who baptizes with the Holy Spirit.' And I have seen and testified that this is the Son of God."
>
> —John 1:29–34, emphasis added

Did you see that? The Spirit—the same as in Old Testament days—came and *remained* on Jesus. Jesus is our prototype. If the Spirit remained on Jesus, we want the Spirit to remain on us.

Not long after that, Jesus spoke about this new reality in His life, which was meant for all humanity:

> And as His [Jesus'] custom was, He went into the synagogue on the Sabbath day, and stood up to read. And He was handed the book of the prophet Isaiah. And when He had opened the book, He found the place where it was written:
>
> "The Spirit of the Lord is upon Me, because He has anointed Me to preach the gospel to the poor; He has sent Me to heal the brokenhearted, to proclaim liberty to the captives and recovery of sight to the blind, to set at liberty those who are oppressed; to proclaim the acceptable year of the Lord."
>
> Then He closed the book, and gave *it* back to the attendant and sat down. And the eyes of all who were in the synagogue were fixed on Him. And He began to say to them, "Today this Scripture is fulfilled in your hearing." So all bore witness to Him, and marveled at the gracious words which

> proceeded out of His mouth. And they said, "Is this not Joseph's son?"
>
> —Luke 4:16–22

It's no surprise they wondered deeply about this because Jesus claimed to be unlike any other person who had ever lived. He was claiming to walk in the continuing power and presence of the Holy Spirit.

He then went on to demonstrate, day by day, what that Spirit-filled life looks like. It is powerful, amazing, spiritually dominant, graceful, wise, miraculous, kind, and so much more.

Many have asked why Jesus didn't stay on earth, drive evil away, and rule justly. The mind-blowing answer is that He wanted you and me to experience the Holy Spirit the same way He did! He told His disciples, and by extension, all of us: "Nevertheless I tell you the truth. It is to your advantage that I go away; for if I do not go away, the Helper will not come to you; but if I depart, I will send Him to you" (John 16:7).

Jesus is the prototype for all Christians, including you and me. He wants us to walk, talk, serve, and love as He did. And to do that, we need a deep and powerful relationship with the Holy Spirit, just as He has. When we give our lives to Jesus, He opens our spirits so we can receive the fullness of the Spirit of God as He did. He was the first to walk in the permanent presence and power of the Holy Spirit, but He was not meant to be the last.

Before going away, Jesus used His last words with His disciples to talk about the Holy Spirit.

> But you shall receive power when the Holy Spirit has come upon you; and you shall be witnesses to Me in Jerusalem, and in all Judea and Samaria, and to the end of the earth." Now when He had spoken these things, while they watched, He was taken up, and a cloud received Him out of their sight.
>
> —ACTS 1:8–9

Picture that! Jesus' final words before ascending to heaven emphasized the critical importance of receiving power "when the Holy Spirit has come upon you" as it came on Him at His water baptism. Like the disciples, we must heed this instruction. He is our prototype and example. We can't say, "I'm OK without that aspect of the Christian life," and expect to live as Jesus did. Honestly, I don't believe we can live as Christians today without the power of the Holy Spirit in our lives.

Reflections for Further Study

1. What has been your experience or history in understanding the Holy Spirit?

2. Spend some time reading through the Book of Acts. Do you see things differently now that you know and are learning about the ministry of the Holy Spirit in a believer's life?

3. Have you ever felt guided or warned by the Holy Spirit about something that happened in your life? Tell about it.

4. What part of your life do you need the most help in? Ask the Holy Spirit to begin to help, and journal about what happens.

CHAPTER 2

THE NORDSTROM CLERK

I LIKE TO SHOP in the men's department at Nordstrom. When I do, I always admire how the employees remain inconspicuous yet present and available. It's a fine balance to strike. They get paid to be discreetly aware of customers' needs, keeping an eye on those who may need help and gently offering assistance at times. Now and then, one of them walks over and says, "Can I help you?" If you say no, the associate smiles and says, "Great. If you need anything, I'll be right over there." Then he walks away and folds shirts or taps on a computer until you have a question. These people are always close enough to help when you ask for it, but they also don't get in your way.

That's a simple but accurate picture of the Holy Spirit. He chooses to be inconspicuous but is always available when we call. He won't shove His way in and tell us what to do. Rather, He stands by and sometimes approaches us to say, "May I help you?"

Amazingly, the Holy Spirit is all-powerful, all-knowing, and completely God but chooses not to intrude where He is not invited.

Why does He behave this way? Because God places great value on our freely given love. He doesn't want automatic, robotic love. Rather, He wants us to experience and express our desire for a relationship with Him. He is a passionate, authentic Being. Like us, He wants to be loved authentically. If He wanted, He could force or manipulate people to want Him more—but that wouldn't be real love. He wants our hearts to choose Him voluntarily, so He gives us complete freedom and does not try to *wow* us into a relationship with Him. He wants our love more than He wants to impress us.

Being under His influence does not mean we are overpowered and out of control.

So, like a well-mannered store associate, the Holy Spirit, our companion and helper, waits to be wanted. Even His name—*parakletos* in the original Greek (the New Testament was originally written in Greek; the Old Testament was originally written in Hebrew)—tells us He is the One who walks beside us; the literal definition is the "one who walks beside."[1] He is always there but does not force Himself into our decisions. He leaves room for us to choose Him, and then He waits.

Awakened to the Voice

Like that store associate, there are times when the Holy Spirit approaches politely and says, "May I help you?" A friend of mine named Jim grew up as a military kid and moved around a lot. His family attended church, but Jim dropped the habit when he got older. He went off to college and felt he was supposed to go to church but neglected to follow through until a friend invited him one week. Jim then started attending regularly.

At a series of church services that went all week long, Jim was impressed by how the minister called people to the front of the church to receive salvation on the last night. The following Wednesday evening at church, Jim's pastor did the same thing, calling people to the front of the church to give their lives to Jesus. Jim turned to his buddy and said, "I'm so glad the pastor is doing altar calls now. He should do them every week."

The friend looked at Jim with puzzlement and said, "He does them every week."

Jim realized he had been sitting through calls to salvation for years but never really noticed them until he began to respond to the Holy Spirit working in his life. It was like he had opened the door to receive help—and the Holy Spirit came near and called his attention to something important. As a result, Jim committed himself to Jesus Christ in a fresh way. His life has never been the same since.

That's a good picture of how the Holy Spirit behaves toward us. He knows when we're ready to see or hear something. It may seem like this truth has been hidden, but it has always been there. We just needed the enlightening presence of our helper to show us.

This explains why some people claim to want to hear from God or know God better, but nothing changes in their lives. Their hearts and mouths are not aligned. The truth is, God is not absent—these people lack readiness. They don't desire God and wouldn't respond favorably if He drew near to them. So He waits. At the right time, the Holy Spirit steps up and says, "May I help you?" He sheds light on some circumstance or truth and gives us the opportunity to respond.

He perfectly perceives when we are willing to partner with Him and take the next steps in our journey with God.

The Night I Met the Helper

I knew nothing about the Holy Spirit when I was a kid, but I did know about being under the influence of alcohol or drugs.

I was the only child of a single mom who liked to party. My mom was heavily involved in drugs, and I had access to whatever substance I wanted. When I wanted to get drunk at age eleven or twelve, my mom said, "Yeah, you can drink as long as I buy the alcohol for you." So I started drinking at that age. I remember my first beer. I remember the first time I smoked a joint. I remember the first time I took speed. I remember the first time I took cocaine. Those were the mile markers in my life. Church, God, and the Bible were nowhere in the picture. I like to make the joke I was "a good pagan."

Just for the record, there is no comparison between being under the influence of alcohol or drugs and being under the influence of the Holy Spirit. They are universes apart from each other. And there are no hangovers with the Holy Spirit.

When I was a young boy, my mom dropped me off at my grandparents' house on the weekends so she could party without worrying about me. That meant I went with my grandparents to church on Sunday morning. As you might expect, I didn't like church. I liked being at the apartment complex where Mom and I lived because my friends and I could run around and do anything we wanted, whenever we wanted. If we felt like riding skateboards, we did that. If we wanted to ride our bikes ten miles away to play video games at the bowling alley, we did that. My life had no rules except when I was at my grandparents' house.

At church I befriended the pastor's son, and he and I would go across the street to play video games and eat candy, using the ten dollars my grandmother gave me to put in the offering plate. (Don't worry, I have repented since then.) We made sure to come back to church right at the end when they were singing the doxology. That was my experience of church from the time I was eight until I graduated high school.

Things changed for me in college when I met a girl named Penny Compton. I wanted to date her, but she wouldn't even give me the time of day. I followed her around the campus after meeting her at my fraternity's party. I would "bump into her" all the time. (I think they call it stalking now!) I finally wore her down, and she said we could go out as friends. We didn't know at the time that the Holy Spirit was setting all this up. Soon she would be Penny Maxwell!

She was not interested in a relationship with some crazy frat boy. After a few dates, I could tell she was very distant, so I took her to my favorite park in Richmond, Virginia. When I asked her why she was not interested, she said something that may as well have been in another language: "I want a guy who's on fire for God." I had no idea what it meant to be on fire for God. It made no sense to me.

"I don't even know what that means," I said and added, "But you haven't even given me a chance."

Her reply was instantaneous: "You haven't gone to church with me."

Having grown up attending church—or, rather, skipping church with the pastor's son to play video games—when my grandparents brought me, I didn't see this as a problem.

"That's all she wants?" I thought. "That's easy. I can do that for a girl."

Churches all seemed the same to me, like ice cream.

They may have had different flavors, but they were all ice cream. Little did I know that churches have significant differences. Some are dead; some are alive. Some welcome the presence and activity of the Holy Spirit, and others don't. So I went to a church service with Penny. It was something that I had never experienced. Yes, it was very different. They didn't have pews. They didn't have an organ. People were lifting their hands and singing. The pastor was energetic, and what he said seemed to hit me right in the center of my chest.

My life started to change over a few weeks of coming. I went every time the doors were open, Sunday morning, Sunday night, and Wednesday night. One Sunday night in November of 1990, a young man named Dennis Rouse was preaching. He had been Penny's youth pastor, and he was getting ready to start his own church in Atlanta, so this was his last night speaking there. I don't remember what he talked about, but I knew God had been dealing with me that month about my behavior, my future, and my very soul. By this time, I was twenty-one years old and addicted to alcohol. I also did a lot of drugs. I was hooked on pornography. Those things had taken over my life, and though it looked like I was having fun, inside, I was desperate to change.

At the end of the service, Pastor Dennis said, "If you want to receive the baptism in the Holy Spirit, I want you to come forward."

I didn't know what "baptism in the Holy Spirit" meant. When it comes to knowing who the Holy Spirit is, I was about a one on a scale of one to ten. I knew we sang about Him in the doxology at the end of my grandparents' church services. But even with all my ignorance, I had a powerful need to make a positive change in my life. The next thing I knew, I was walking down the middle of the aisle. We were sitting about fifteen rows back, and before I reached the front, I felt an unknown language burst out of my mouth in an unstoppable way. It was something I had never experienced before.

"What on earth is going on?" I wondered as the floodgates of this unknown language opened wide. I would read later in the Bible that Jesus said living water would flow from your belly, but at the time, I had no grid for what was occurring. I think God sneaked up on me through my own ignorance and need because I probably wouldn't have been open had I known analytically and logically what I was getting into. I was coming under the influence of the Holy Spirit.

I knelt at the front of the auditorium, and the rest of that evening was a blur—a good blur. This incredible language kept rushing out of me, and the sense of God's presence was almost overwhelming. Just as amazing was the cleansing that took place in my life. Within a few weeks, my alcohol, drug, and pornography habits completely disappeared. My desires changed, and I fell in love with the Bible. My fraternity brothers and college friends didn't recognize me—and, truthfully, I hardly recognized myself. But I liked what I saw.

So did Penny. We were married two years later and served in many ways over the next twelve years in that church, helping to build a youth group and seeing hundreds of lives changed and many young people start their journey and ministry in the kingdom of God. I preached in prisons, took overseas trips, and held open-air meetings in third-world countries. Then in 2002, Penny, our three kids, and I moved to Charlotte, North Carolina, to start Freedom House church, where we are now.

Think for a moment about the timing of what happened to me. The Holy Spirit is sovereign. He could have blindside-tackled me at any time in my life and saved me a lot of headaches and heartaches. He could have intervened when I was a rebellious kid in my grandparents' church. He could have stopped me from falling into various addictions. He could have done anything—but He was waiting for me to take a step toward Him. The Bible says, "Draw near to God and He will draw near to you" (Jas. 4:8). Notice who does the first "drawing." Relationships are all about drawing near to each other repeatedly.

If you have been a Christian for a while but are not in the same place you once were with God, ask yourself: who moved? I can tell you that God is waiting for you to move so He can move.

When you step toward the Holy Spirit, He steps toward you, and often it's unexpectedly powerful and life-transforming.

The Holy Spirit Speaks

Now that I was walking under the influence of the Holy Spirit, He guided me—sometimes in ways I never saw coming.

At the time, I was on the verge of graduating from college, and my dream was to make a bunch of money. I grew up poor, so the idea of being able to make a good living was important to me. Because I had invited the Holy Spirit into my life, He could teach me whatever He wanted—and He started with the subject of money.

I was sitting in the second row of the church I attended with my wife, Penny, listening to a man speak about giving. He was telling amazing stories of miracles he had witnessed, some of which involved finances. Then a voice behind me spoke audibly and said, "You need to listen to this story."

I turned around to see who had said it. The guy sitting in the chair behind me looked at me blankly as if to say, "What do you want?"

"Did you say something to me?" I asked. He shook his head and arched an eyebrow like I might be crazy. So I turned back around.

A few seconds later, the voice spoke again: "You need to listen to this story."

I turned around again, but it was clear the guy hadn't said anything. I had heard the voice of God, and He was saying to listen and learn about this principle of giving.

I obeyed that voice, bought a bunch of books on money, and devoured all the Bible teaching on giving that I could find. I learned the biblical view of tithing, giving, and the proper place and use of finances in my life. Money had become a god to me then. I had to dethrone money to make way for God to rule in my life.

That was the work of the Holy Spirit. He broke me free from the love of money, which is a prison, and helped me fall in love with the Bible. I still love it to this day. I had drawn near to Him, and He was drawing near to me.

That was the beginning of my journey of living under the influence of the Holy Spirit, and though I couldn't see it at the time, I was heading to a place where I needed to study deeply for myself what the Bible says about the work of the Holy Spirit. That required letting go of old paradigms and limitations and letting the Scriptures teach me anew who this helper is, what He wants to do, and how to partner with Him.

Heavenly Father, what areas of my life do I need to have Your Spirit deal with? I am asking You to guide me in dethroning any idols that have become stumbling blocks to my relationship with You, God. Lead me and teach me. In Jesus' name, amen.

Reflections for Further Study

1. Describe your experience with the Holy Spirit thus far. How would you describe His character and behavior with you?

2. How does your upbringing affect your view of the Holy Spirit's work? What did your church or community teach, if anything, about the Holy Spirit? How does this affect your viewpoint now?

3. When was the first time you heard the term *baptism in the Holy Spirit*? What came to mind when you heard it? What was your emotional reaction to it?

4. Was there a time when God encountered you in a special way? Describe that here. Was it powerful? Convicting? Comforting? Revealing? All the above?

5. Consider the following account of the Holy Spirit guiding a Christian named Philip to share the gospel with a high-ranking government leader. Have you ever felt guided, and perhaps surprised, by something God did? How did you react? What was the outcome? Explain here.

A man of Ethiopia, a eunuch of great authority under Candace the queen of the Ethiopians, who had charge of all her treasury, and had come to Jerusalem to worship, was returning. And sitting in his chariot, he was reading Isaiah the prophet. Then the Spirit said to Philip, "Go near and overtake this chariot." So Philip ran to him, and heard him reading the prophet Isaiah, and said, "Do you understand what you are reading?"

And he said, "How can I, unless someone guides me?" And he asked Philip to come up and sit with him. . . .

Then Philip opened his mouth, and beginning at this Scripture, preached Jesus to him. Now as they went down the road, they came to some water. And the eunuch said, "See, here is water. What hinders me from being baptized?"

Then Philip said, "If you believe with all your heart, you may."

And he answered and said, "I believe that Jesus Christ is the Son of God."

So he commanded the chariot to stand still. And both Philip and the eunuch went down into the water, and he baptized him. Now when they came up out of the water, the Spirit of the Lord caught Philip away, so that the eunuch saw him no more; and he went on his way rejoicing.

—Acts 8:27–31, 35–39

CHAPTER 3

THE HOLY SPIRIT ISN'T WEIRD; PEOPLE ARE

PENNY AND I were pursuing God with all our might as a young married couple. The Holy Spirit's influence had transformed my life even before I understood who He is or what was happening to me. I took a step toward Him, and He took a big step toward me—and everything changed for the better. Not only did Penny now have a guy who was "on fire for God," but all my priorities did a one-eighty. We began going to church together all the time. In fact, we became super-volunteers, spending dozens of hours a week to help build the church in just about every area.

It was a great season for us personally and in ministry. We were learning and growing in ways that were exciting and new.

Our church welcomed the activity of the Holy Spirit in its services, and I witnessed the power of God at work so many times. It was beyond exciting to watch people receive healing from disease and sickness and witness people coming out of wheelchairs or receiving their hearing. I have to also mention the many lives impacted by the restoration of marriages and entire families. Church was far from boring. Rather, it was the most life-giving, fun, and powerful environment I had ever experienced.

While the church was dynamic, growing, and open to the activity of the Holy Spirit, over time, human dynamics kicked in at the leadership level—yes, that happens in churches, too—and the church community fractured. A somewhat toxic atmosphere set in, and many people soon felt burned by some sad situations. Penny and I were among those who saw things that we now realize were not healthy. It was a great leadership lesson and helped us not to repeat those same behaviors when we became pastors.

Allow me to interject something here about church. It is not a perfect place because it is overseen by imperfect people. If you have been through tough times in a church, don't give up on it. Learn from it. Believe the best in people. Leave in a way that honors others if you need to, and always trust God.

Why share a "negative" report like this? Because I

know some people reading this book will have had bad experiences in churches, even churches that valued the presence and influence of the Holy Spirit. The danger in the aftermath of those situations is to let disillusionment and bitterness take root (Heb. 12:15). Some people push God away. That's a predictable response but not a healthy one. Others slam the door on "that type of church," whatever it was, and choose a new church that is the opposite of the old one. They might nurture wounds and justify bad attitudes about what took place before. They're afraid of being hurt again.

The truth is that every church, movement, and denomination has real problems. Bad experiences are unavoidable. If we throw the baby out with the bath water, we are left with nothing. We must learn to hold on to valuable things and let go of those that aren't. Major on the major and minor on the minor. If we're not careful, we can stop the work of God in our lives. It's easy to become offended and wall off what God is trying to do in our lives.

Because I had known just one church in my Christian life, the trouble there could have shipwrecked my faith big time. Penny and I could have walked away from ministry influenced and led by the Holy Spirit because we felt hurt or used by people. But instead, by God's grace, we chose to pick up the pieces and move forward in health and forgiveness. That decision, to my surprise, led me to a new, better understanding of the Holy Spirit.

God burdened our hearts to start a church in Charlotte, North Carolina. We had no connections there, and neither of us had ever been there. We sought counsel, prayed a lot, and decided to follow what we believed was the Lord's call to Charlotte.

When I left Richmond, Virginia, I also felt the Lord leading me to do something else I had never done before: give my Bible away. This was a huge deal because I had come to love that Bible and had spent hundreds of hours reading from its pages, marking things, and dwelling on certain passages and words. Your Bible becomes incredibly special to you when you spend a lot of time with it, as many people know. But a season of life was coming to an end, and I wanted a fresh start. It felt right to give it to a young man I had been mentoring, and it meant a lot to him as well.

I planned to buy a new Bible and read it cover to cover specifically to start a fresh relationship with the Father, Jesus, His son, and the Holy Spirit. I wanted to understand the Holy Spirit biblically, not just experientially in a certain way influenced at a certain church. I wasn't turning my back on what the Holy Spirit had done before; I was saying yes to what He had next.

Before I bought my next Bible, members of our new team in Charlotte gave me one as a gift. I told God, "I'm going to read the whole Book, from Genesis to Revelation, because I want to start this journey with You afresh. Holy Spirit, speak to me through the Scriptures as I read. Help me to understand You and Your work." I knew it was an important decision, but I couldn't yet see how life-changing it would be.

Though I felt I had studied the Holy Spirit and His

role so extensively that there wasn't much else to learn, now I saw new things, deeper things, more aspects of how the Holy Spirit works, and why we need His power, influence, and peace in our lives. He laid a strong, biblical foundation in my heart so I could understand what happens when we come under His influence. It made a huge difference going forward, and I want to share it with you step by step and firmly rooted in what the Bible teaches.

The Three Baptisms

The first foundational truth I saw is that there are three baptisms for the believer. This surprised me, as it may surprise you. Many Christians have only heard of one or two of these baptisms. We typically think of baptism as water baptism; even the dictionary defines *baptism* as "a Christian sacrament marked by ritual use of water."[1] But the Bible clearly speaks of three distinct baptisms:

1. Salvation = First Baptism
2. Water = Second Baptism
3. Baptism in the Holy Spirit = Third Baptism

Let's look to Scripture for an understanding of this.

> Therefore, leaving the discussion of the elementary principles of Christ, let us go on to perfection, not laying again the foundation of repentance from dead works and of faith toward God, of the doctrine of *baptisms*, of laying on of hands, of

> resurrection of the dead, and of eternal judgment. And this we will do if God permits.
>
> —HEBREWS 6:1–3, EMPHASIS ADDED

Notice that the word *baptisms* in the middle of that passage is plural. Not one baptism but more than one. This verse is not referring to multiple water baptisms. Rather, it means we undergo more than one baptism in our walk of faith.

Let's put this in context as we unpack the passage. The writer of Hebrews says that every believer should understand the "elementary principles of Christ." These are not exotic or mysterious teachings but foundational principles of the Christian faith. He essentially says, "We'll talk about basic principles if time permits, but we really need to get past them and on to maturity." It's as if he's telling us we should be in high school or college courses by now, but instead, we're stuck in grade school, spiritually speaking. Among these basic principles—these grade-school topics—are these baptisms he refers to.

It can be humbling for Christians to look at this list and these baptisms and admit we don't fully understand them yet. But the Bible warns us for a reason, and we must take the correction seriously and let the Bible measure us rather than the other way around.

If you look around you at the state of the church, as wonderful as the people are and as exciting as we may find our activities and growth, we have to confess a certain shallowness in our collective knowledge of the

Bible. Many sincere Christians are stuck in a state of immaturity, unfamiliar with "the elementary principles of Christ." God urges us to master these things and move forward.

Elsewhere in the letter, the writer of Hebrews scolds his readers for still requiring "milk" when they should be on to "solid food" (Heb. 5:12). If you ever feel bored or blasé about your Christian walk, it may be because God wants you to enjoy some meat, but you're still learning to digest milk! We must keep progressing, or we'll stall at one stage or another. It's time for Christians to accelerate out of the beginning stages and level-up in our understanding.

A critical component of this is to understand what he means by *baptisms.*

> *Father, I want to go deep in my relationship with You. I want more of the meat of Your word. Open my heart and mind to hear Your voice, take the shovel of curiosity, and dig deep into Your word. In Jesus' name, amen.*

Before we go into each type of baptism, it's important to understand the word itself and what a Mideastern mind might conceptualize when they see the word *baptism.* The first concept is like dying a piece of cloth a different color, meaning a complete change from one disposition to another. The cloth would be so completely changed that it would be unrecognizable. For example, it was once yellow and is now green. It has been *baptized.*

A second concept represented by the word *baptism* would be a ship on the ocean that sunk, and now the water is in the ship. The ship was not just immersed but completely overtaken by the water it once floated on. Instead of the ship being *on* the water, the water is now *in* the ship. The ship has been *baptized.*

A third concept for baptism would be a piece of food dipped in something to change the taste or add flavor that wasn't there. Like you take a tortilla chip and put it in some queso. It tasted one way and now tastes different. The chip was *baptized.*

OK, now we have a good picture of what someone should see when they think of baptism. You aren't just immersed; you are changed. You don't just go on living the same way; after this experience, you are never the same again. Everything is different. With that in mind, let's examine how each type of baptism affects your life.

The Baptism of Salvation

The first baptism is familiar to all Christians because it is a baptism into salvation. Today, there is such an emphasis on salvation that it almost overshadows the other baptisms that follow it. But many people don't know that the Bible refers to salvation as baptism: "For by one Spirit we were all baptized into one body—whether Jews or Greeks, whether slaves or free—and have all been made to drink into one Spirit" (1 Cor. 12:13).

Paul is saying that the first baptism—salvation—unites us with Christ, and we go from being isolated, unredeemed individuals to belonging to God's own family. Because of what Jesus did for us on the cross, we now have an unblemished relationship with our heavenly Father. He calls this profound change a baptism because it transforms our lives and marks a major passage from one reality to another. Indeed, it is such a huge change that the apostle John calls it the difference between life and death.

So who baptizes us into salvation? Most people reflexively say Jesus, but the answer is the Holy Spirit does. "For by *one Spirit* we were all baptized into one body" (v. 13, emphasis added). Without the Holy Spirit, you and I would not be saved. The Holy Spirit shows us we need a Savior, Jesus. The Holy Spirit convicts us of our sin and draws every believer to salvation in Jesus. The same Holy Spirit baptizes us into the body of Christ at the time of salvation. Jesus did the work; the Holy Spirit testifies to it in our hearts.

And, of course, the helper's work does not end there. Paul writes that the Holy Spirit bears witness with our spirit that we belong to God—that we are His children (Rom. 8:16). In other words, He gives us confidence in our baptism into the body of Christ. When we are tempted to doubt it, He says, "No, trust me: you're saved." When you make a mistake and repent, He reassures you, "You are still saved. Don't doubt that you belong to God's family."

In another of Paul's letters, we read that "in Him

[Jesus] you also trusted, after you heard the word of truth, the gospel of your salvation; in whom also, having believed, you were sealed with the Holy Spirit of promise" (Eph. 1:13). The word *sealed* is our reassurance and guarantee. It means it's a done deal. You can't fall off the back of the truck by accident. The Holy Spirit has your back at all times. He has baptized you into the body of Christ and has sealed your salvation. That is the first baptism we experience as believers.

BAPTISM IN WATER

The second baptism is in water. It is an outward expression of what happened to us on the inside when the Holy Spirit baptized us into salvation. We were dirty on the inside—unrighteous and separated from God—until God's mercy is given to us by God's grace. He not only cleans us up but stands sinless before the Father on our behalf. Water baptism is an outward picture and public declaration of our transference from death to life through the baptism of salvation. It is symbolic and easy to understand—a living picture of our becoming a brand-new person in Christ. Let me make it super simple. Water baptism washes you of your old life.

Water baptism accomplishes a couple of very important things. It serves as a milestone and foundation stone in our spiritual walk. Meaningful emotions accompany it as we engage in a powerful moment in front of other people and the Lord. It also strengthens our community by creating witnesses who remember our commitment and hold us accountable to our public declaration. So water baptism serves the body on an individual and community level.

Let me ask you, Who does the baptizing in water? The answer is simple yet easily overlooked: disciples of Jesus Christ do the baptizing. A disciple is anyone who is a believer and has decided to follow Jesus. We know this because Jesus instructed His followers, "Go therefore and make disciples of all the nations, baptizing them in the name of the Father and of the Son and of the Holy Spirit" (Matt. 28:19). Baptizing people in water is not a privilege reserved for the first apostles, disciples, or the spiritual elite. Nor is it only for ordained ministers, pastors, deacons, elders or "spiritual professionals" today. Any disciple of Christ can do it. If you are a born-again believer, you have the authority to baptize someone in water, according to the words of Jesus.

At our church we dedicate a specific Sunday, and at all our campuses we put big tanks at the front. During our time of worship at the beginning of the service we have people baptized in front of the whole church. Their family, friends and all the people who have watched their life transform get to participate in this amazing moment. Something really special that we also do is allow fathers to baptize their kids. The faces of both the fathers and children is priceless. They are investing into their children's lives in a way that will make spiritual memories they will never forget.

We see this in Acts 8, where a Christian disciple named Philip talked with a man, led him to faith in

Christ, and baptized him in water right by the side of the road! Philip didn't call back to Jerusalem to have an apostle come down. He was empowered as a disciple of Jesus to baptize another believer. And he did.

Salvation and water baptism are the first two baptisms. So far, so good. Now let's look at the least understood—and most contentious—baptism of all.

HOLY SPIRIT BAPTISM

Most Christians agree about the baptisms into salvation and in water—but many Christians do not like to talk about the third baptism, and many would rather sidestep and ignore it altogether. People often say, "When I got saved, I received the Holy Spirit." Or, "That baptism was for a certain group of people at a certain time, and we don't have that anymore." Or, "When I got saved, I got everything I needed. Christ is all-sufficient."

Those phrases can all sound high-minded and Christ-honoring, and each is true in part, but too many Christians use such arguments to dismiss this third baptism altogether. Again, let's look to the Word as our guide and take our study step by step, never departing from biblical teaching. *What I love about the Bible is once you see it, you will never unsee it.* The baptism in the Holy Spirit is spoken of in all four Gospels, specifically in Matthew 3:11, Mark 1:8, Luke 3:16, and John 1:33, which are listed below. Remember that each one of these accounts is written by a different person. Very few things are related in all four Gospels, but the baptism in the Holy Spirit is one of them. These passages read as follows, and I have italicized the part of each verse that is relevant to this teaching.

- "I indeed baptize you with water unto repentance, but He who is coming after me is mightier than I, whose sandals I am not worthy to carry. *He will baptize you with the Holy Spirit and fire*" (Matt. 3:11).
- "I indeed baptized you with water, *but He will baptize you with the Holy Spirit*" (Mark 1:8).
- "John answered, saying to all, 'I indeed baptize you with water; but One mightier than I is coming, whose sandal strap I am not worthy to loose. *He will baptize you with the Holy Spirit and fire*'" (Luke 3:16).
- "I did not know Him, but He who sent me to baptize with water said to me, 'Upon whom you see the Spirit descending, and remaining on Him, *this is He who baptizes with the Holy Spirit*'" (John 1:33).

Notice that the baptism in the Holy Spirit showed up even before Jesus' ministry started, and it was spoken through the lips of John the Baptist at the beginning of each Gospel account. It is something that all four writers of the Gospels felt was necessary to include in their portrayal of the life of Jesus. This third baptism was central to the ministry of Jesus and the lives of His followers. It wasn't tacked on to the gospel as an optional bonus experience. It wasn't going to be a one-and-done scenario on the day of Pentecost. Rather, the promise of this third baptism was a key part of Jesus' ministry and was important enough that John foretold it as a confirming sign of who the Messiah would be.

Before we dive into what this baptism is, let me pose several valid questions many people have: Did Jesus experience these three baptisms? Was Jesus "saved"? Did Jesus have to be born again, as we do? Was He baptized in the Holy Spirit?

These questions may sound funny, but many people wonder about them. Let's look to the Bible for answers. First, was Jesus saved? Was there some remnant of original sin in Him from Mary's side, and did Jesus have to be born again like the rest of us?

The answer is no; Jesus was never born again because He was born right the first time! Jesus was born perfect and inherited none of the sinful nature of our forefather, Adam, through Mary. While you and I need to be baptized into right standing with the Father, Jesus was born in right standing with the Father from the very beginning. We can say with confidence that He fulfilled this first baptism upon conception. He was already "saved" without any implication that He needed saving from sin because He was sinless then, now, and forever.

What about the second baptism (water)? Most people know that Jesus was baptized in water by His cousin, John the Baptist. Remember, fellow believers can perform water baptism, but even so, John protested, saying, in essence, "I'm not worthy of doing this. You should baptize me!" But Jesus knew that God planned to make Him a prototype for humanity in all three baptisms, so Jesus told John he had to do this to fulfill all righteousness.

How about the third baptism? Was Jesus baptized in the Holy Spirit? Yes, and it happened right after He was baptized in water. God had told John the Baptist that this would happen. John testified, "He who sent me to baptize with water said to me, 'Upon whom you see the Spirit descending, and *remaining on Him, this is He*" (John 1:33, emphasis added).

That's exactly what happened. As Jesus was coming out of the water, the Bible says the Spirit of God descended upon Him—and then something unprecedented happened: the Holy Spirit remained on Him. This detail is monumentally important for us to understand.

Until this point in history, the Holy Spirit had never remained on anybody. All through the Old Testament, the Holy Spirit came upon people and then lifted. He came upon Samson, empowered him mightily, then lifted. He rested upon Joshua, Gideon, David, Elijah, Elisha, and many others—but always lifted after accomplishing a specific task or mission. The Holy Spirit never remained on a person—until Jesus came.

Why could the Holy Spirit not remain on people before? Because their human spirits were not reconciled to God. Nobody on earth was born again. Sin still corrupted their spirits. Jesus came to remove that corruption and make a way for us to receive everything God had for us from the beginning—including the empowering Holy Spirit. This is why we must be baptized into salvation before we are baptized in the Holy Spirit. He only remains in a cleansed vessel, and only Jesus makes us clean before the Father.

I imagine the "cloud of witnesses" (Heb. 12:1) watching Jesus' baptism in the waters of the Jordan River that day. What made it so exciting was that the Holy Spirit would settle on Jesus and remain there. I believe every Old Testament saint and prophet peered over the gates of heaven to see what they had talked about, written about, prophesied about, and even seen visions about. Finally, the Messiah had come to receive all the promises they had foretold and do extraordinary things no other man could do—and it began with His baptism in the Holy Spirit.

Up to this point, Jesus had done no public ministry. His ministry began when the Holy Spirit remained on Him. Was Jesus any less the Son of God before that? No. But, like us, He needed to undergo this third baptism to accomplish the specific works the Father had designed for Him. It was necessary for Jesus to experience all three baptisms.

So it is vitally necessary for us to experience them as well.

A Baptism of Power

The baptism with the Holy Spirit is, perhaps foremost, a baptism of power. It enables you to do and be everything God planned for your life. This power is not just for ministry activities; it is the power to resist temptation, avoid addiction, ward off anxious thoughts, serve others, and be the husband, wife, or single person God has called you to be. Without Holy Spirit baptism, we live far below our full potential. We need this baptism of power in our culture today. We are all called as Christians to be a light in a very dark world.

Think of Jesus' example. As soon as He was baptized in the Holy Spirit, "the Spirit drove him into the wilderness" to resist temptation for forty days while fasting (Mark 1:12). He was alone but for the wild animals, angels, and, of course, Satan, who offered up one temptation after another to no avail. Then Jesus emerged in the power of the Holy Spirit and began His public ministry (Luke 4:14). Before receiving this third baptism, Jesus did no public miracles. He didn't pray for anybody, didn't cast out any devils, or restore blind eyes, deaf ears, or mute tongues. Though He was perfect and sinless, His ministry only started when He received the baptism in the Holy Spirit.

This explains why there's so much controversy and confusion surrounding the third baptism. It's powerful! The devil does not want you or me operating in power. His worst nightmare is a Christian who wakes up fully *under the influence* of the Holy Spirit because they have been baptized in the Holy Spirit. Our enemy does not want us to live with the strength to deal with temptations, demons, and any problem the evil world presents. His strategy is to deceive and confuse us about the third baptism, so people leave it alone and say, "I don't quite get it, so I'll get along without it." That is the recipe for a powerless church with powerless people sitting in it.

Don't Go Until You Wait

Let me be clear about what I'm saying: a church that embraces the first two baptisms but rejects or wrongly defines the third baptism will be powerless. It will be powerless because only the Holy Spirit can accomplish through us the greater works the gospel requires. Let me illustrate this the best way I know how. Have you ever tried to cut down a tree? I have used a chainsaw, an axe, and a saw. All three work. You could cut down a tree with a butter knife with enough time and effort. The best way to cut down a tree is with a chainsaw. It cuts through the wood with little effort. I've never tried to use a butter knife to cut down a tree, but I imagine it would take a few days, if not weeks. I would much rather have the chainsaw.

As a Christian, would you rather go into life with a chainsaw or a butter knife? I know what God wants for us! He wants us to have His power, the power of the Holy Spirit, to deal with anything we face.

Yet many new disciples of Jesus jump right into their Christian life without ever being baptized in the Holy

Spirit. They want to get into the Great Commission and make disciples, teach, or serve. But they miss the critical third baptism Jesus requires. Christians usually think Jesus' last command was to make disciples of all the nations in Matthew 28:19. But that's not true. Jesus' final command before ascending to heaven was, "Behold, I send the Promise of My Father upon you; but tarry in the city of Jerusalem until you are endued with power from on high" (Luke 24:49).

Tarry means to wait. So the last command Jesus gave His disciples was not, "Go," but "Wait." Specifically, wait "until you are endued with power from on high." This lines up with something else Jesus said, "for He [the Holy Spirit] dwells with you and will be in you" (John 14:17). Notice Jesus refers to two distinct moments there. The Holy Spirit already "dwells with you," but one day "will be in you." Look also at His teaching here, parts of which I italicized for emphasis.

> And being assembled together with them, He commanded them not to depart from Jerusalem, but to *wait for the Promise of the Father*, "which," He said, "you have heard from Me; for John truly baptized with water, *but you shall be baptized* with the Holy Spirit not many days from now." Therefore, when they had come together, they asked Him, saying, "Lord, will You at this time restore the kingdom to Israel?" And He said to them, "It is not for you to know times or seasons which the Father has put in His own authority. But *you shall receive power* when the Holy Spirit

> has come upon you; and *you shall be witnesses* to Me in Jerusalem, and in all Judea and Samaria, and to the end of the earth."
>
> —Acts 1:4–8, emphasis added

Now look at this passage that sheds even more light on this baptism.

> "He who believes in Me, as the Scripture has said, out of his heart will flow rivers of living water." But this He spoke concerning the Spirit, whom those believing in Him would receive; for the Holy Spirit was not yet given, because Jesus was not yet glorified.
>
> —John 7:38–39

John was writing about the baptism in the Holy Spirit, which the disciples later experienced in Acts 2. The sequence of events goes something like this. The disciples got saved after Jesus was raised from the dead because Paul taught "that if you confess with your mouth the Lord Jesus and believe in your heart that God has raised Him from the dead, you will be saved" (Rom. 10:9). We don't know when they were baptized in water, and the order of the second and third baptisms doesn't matter. It only matters that the first baptism happens before the others. So the disciples were born again after Jesus rose from the dead. Then Jesus instructed them to go to Jerusalem to wait for the third baptism.

Clearly, baptism with the Holy Spirit is a separate and distinct experience for the believer. At this point, the disciples were saved. They were going to heaven. They had been taught many things by Jesus and could have taught others, shared the gospel, testified of the risen Christ, and so on. But Jesus disallowed this until they had waited and been baptized in the Holy Spirit. Anyone who insists, "I got everything I needed at the time of salvation," or "I received the Holy Spirit when I was born again," is in biblical error about this third baptism. They simply cannot answer why Jesus would promise another empowering experience, which the Bible vividly describes in Acts 2 and elsewhere. There is no way to push this aside or make it simultaneous with (and indistinguishable from) salvation.

Again, the enemy desperately wants to sow confusion concerning this experience. He wants Christians to believe that salvation is the same as receiving the Holy Spirit. This effectively cancels the power of the Christian life. The devil will make that deal all day long. He wants Christians to think, as many already do, "Why do I need the baptism in the Holy Spirit? Nobody at my church talks about it. I hear conflicting teaching about it. I've done OK so far without it. I'll leave it alone and stick with salvation and the Bible."

If the disciples had done that, there would be no church today. The church was born in the power of the Holy Spirit on the day Jesus baptized His followers with the Holy Spirit in Jerusalem. There, they spoke in tongues for the first time as the Spirit gave them the flow of words. There, the Spirit drew onlookers and piqued their curiosity over what was happening. There, the Spirit emboldened Peter to preach an amazing message of repentance to a potentially hard-hearted crowd. There, the Spirit convicted those hearts and brought three thousand people to repentance.

What if the disciples had said after Jesus ascended, "We're not sure what Jesus was talking about with that Holy Spirit stuff. It doesn't make sense to us. We saw the risen Christ and the empty tomb. We remember the gospel message and His teachings. Let's skip this other experience and start evangelizing the world. We can get along without this other baptism."

The truth is, some did that. Of the five hundred Jesus told to wait, three hundred and eighty failed to obey. Some may have faded because they wanted Jesus to immediately restore the kingdom of Israel, as we see in Acts 1. But that wasn't the plan. Others probably went to the upper room but gave up waiting for the promise because they got impatient, disgruntled, or bored—who knows? Maybe conflicts broke out among some of them. Maybe others had business or family obligations they sneaked away to take care of. Whatever the reasons, only one hundred and twenty remained to wait for the third baptism on the day of Pentecost. Like many in churches today, the great majority didn't wait for the power. They just went ahead with what they had. They went to chopping trees with a butter knife.

To have any power in our "GO," we need to "WAIT" to be baptized in the Holy Spirit. A gospel without power is hardly a gospel at all. Jesus taught that it's not enough to receive salvation and be water-baptized. We need salvation, the Bible, and all these foundations of the Christian life—but we also need Spirit baptism to have power in life and ministry. This is the clear and plain teaching of the Bible.

Can you be saved without experiencing the baptism with the Holy Spirit? Yes, but why would you want to? Why reject what Jesus commanded and the Cross provided for you—a powerful partnering relationship fully under the influence of the Spirit of God? Who wants to live a weak, ineffective life? All Christians possess a measure of the grace of God for living, but Jesus commanded His followers to be baptized in the Holy Spirit as a subsequent experience of salvation. Remember, you wouldn't take a butter knife into a forest aiming to cut down trees. Could you do it? Maybe, but it would take a long time compared to a chainsaw. The third baptism is not a matter of heaven and hell—it is a matter of impact and effectiveness, not to mention the great peace and enjoyment of the Holy Spirit, which are part of this baptism.

It is a baptism Jesus urges you to welcome and experience.

A Different Level of Intimacy

Penny once took a bunch of young ladies to the beach for a spiritual retreat. At one point, she taught about the baptism with the Holy Spirit and invited them to receive it. One young mom, Nichole, had been a Christian and a worship leader for some time but came from a church that didn't teach on the third baptism. As she heard the teaching, she made up her mind and decided to go for it, and she was baptized in the Holy Spirit and began speaking in other tongues—which I'll discuss later.

Nichole later said something that struck me: "For years and years, it felt like there was something inside me that needed to come out," she said. "It felt like it was rising in my throat but wouldn't come out. I knew I should pray in tongues, but I needed someone to teach me why I should. As soon as I had this understanding, the dam was broken, and the words flooded out of me. I began praying in this wonderful language that had been there all the time."

Since that time, Nichole's life has changed dramatically. She has power for living, power for ministry, enjoyment of God, and a deep peace that nothing can take. People say that being baptized in the Holy Spirit is like marrying someone versus dating them. It's a whole different level of intimacy. You experience more, go further, go faster, and enjoy the journey much more when you come under the influence of the wonderful Holy Spirit.

If we sincerely desire everything God wants for us, we will do what Nichole did and open ourselves to receive everything God wants to give us—including this third baptism given to us by Jesus. This wonderful gift we can all enjoy.

Father, I want all three baptisms. I want all You have for me. I believe that Jesus is the Son of God, and He came to set me free from my sins. I believe that He rose from the dead and is now at God's right hand. Jesus is my Savior and my Lord. I believe the Holy Spirit is real, and I want Him to fill me, to baptize me. I ask for His power to flow through me and in me to accomplish His plan for my life. I submit myself to Him now in Jesus' name.

Reflections for Further Study

1. Have you ever had a negative experience involving what was said to be the Holy Spirit at a church? If you're comfortable doing so, describe what happened.

2. How did you respond to that experience? How did it impact your life going forward?

3. Which of the three baptisms—salvation, water baptism, baptism with the Holy Spirit—have you experienced?

4. Do you ever feel like you have stalled in your growth as a Christian? Explain why you felt or feel that way.

5. What, if anything, were you taught about Holy Spirit baptism? What was the most confusing part about what you learned?

6. Are you open to receiving this third baptism? If not, why not?

7. Read and reflect on this passage:

> And I will pray the Father, and He will give you another Helper, that He may abide with you forever—the Spirit of truth, whom the world cannot receive,

> because it neither sees Him nor knows Him; but you know Him, for He dwells with you and will be in you....
>
> These things I have spoken to you while being present with you. But the Helper, the Holy Spirit, whom the Father will send in My name, He will teach you all things, and bring to your remembrance all things that I said to you.
>
> —John 14:16–17, 25–26

8. Jesus said the Spirit would abide with us forever and be in us, would teach us all things and bring Jesus' words to our remembrance. Which of these promises have you experienced in your walk with God?

CHAPTER 4

THREE BAPTISMS THROUGHOUT THE BIBLE

THE THIRD BAPTISM is deeply rooted in Scripture, going back to the very first verses of the Bible. We must see how God laid the foundations for us to experience and walk in the power of the Holy Spirit through the Old and New Testaments. Then we can have confidence that this gift of empowerment and intimacy has been meant for us all along.

The Three Baptisms Foretold in the Old Testament

Have you ever noticed that God often does things in threes? There are three members of the godhead: Father, Son, and Holy Spirit. Jesus rose from the dead on the third day. Jesus turned water into wine on the third day of the wedding. How many years did Jesus minister? Three years. How many days was Jonah in the belly of the whale? Three. On it goes throughout the Bible.

This pattern of threes also shows up in the giving of the baptism in the Holy Spirit. The disciples were baptized in the Holy Spirit on the day of Pentecost, the third of three major Jewish holiday celebrations.

- Passover represents Jesus' death.
- First Fruits represents Jesus' resurrection.
- Pentecost represents Spirit baptism.

Again, God works in threes. When you study it, three seems to represent perfection and unity in a given circumstance.

- There were three patriarchs of Israel: Abraham, Isaac, and Jacob.
- Paul wrote that three things are most important to the believer: faith, hope, and love.

- Our own existence speaks of three: body, soul, and spirit.
- Families are husband, wife, and child (or children).
- The Jewish temple consisted of the outer court, the inner court, and the holy of holies.

These examples represent the unity and perfection inherent in the godhead and in everything God makes and does.

Three in the Beginning

The Bible even starts with the three members of the Trinity interacting: "In the beginning God created the heavens and the earth. The earth was without form, and void; and darkness was on the face of the deep. And the Spirit of God was hovering over the face of the waters. Then God said, 'Let there be light'" (Gen. 1:1–3).

It may not jump out at you in a quick reading, but these verses show the unity and perfection of the Father, Son, and Holy Spirit working actively together. First, God the Father created. Then the Holy Spirit hovered over the not-yet-organized material of creation. Then the Father spoke the Word—Jesus Himself—who flooded the new creation with light. We know from the Gospel of John that Jesus was, is, and ever shall be the Word of God and the Light of the world, and that through Him, all things were made. From the very beginning, God worked in threes.

The Baptisms Prophetically Foretold

More specifically, we see the three baptisms foreshadowed in the Old Testament. Foreshadowing is simply a peek into the future or an indication of something that is to come. The Old Testament will often foreshadow a principle of salvation with a story, and the New Testament will complete that picture with a truth—often, through what Jesus did for us in His sacrifice. This is important because it shows that God always intended us to experience baptism into His family, baptism in water, and baptism with the Holy Spirit. Unfortunately, many Christians conclude that the Old Testament is irrelevant to modern life and can be ignored by those who have "a better covenant" (Heb. 7:22, 8:6). But the New Testament itself tells us that the Old Testament remains fully relevant to our growth as believers. Paul wrote in his letters:

- "For whatever things were written before were written for our learning, that we through the patience and comfort of the Scriptures might have hope" (Rom. 15:4).

- "All Scripture is given by inspiration of God, and is profitable for doctrine, for reproof, for correction, for instruction in righteousness, that the man of God may be complete, thoroughly equipped for every good work" (2 Tim. 3:16–17).

- "Now these things [Old Testament accounts] became our examples, to the intent that we should not lust after evil things as they also lusted" (1 Cor. 10:6).

- The men of Berea, where Paul preached, "searched the Scriptures daily to find out whether these things [which Paul taught] were so." Paul described a disciple named Apollos as "an eloquent man and mighty in the Scriptures," and he "vigorously refuted the Jews publicly, showing from the Scriptures that Jesus is the Christ" (Acts 17:11; 18:24, 28). Numerous times, Paul anchored his teaching to Old Testament, which he called "the prophetic Scriptures made known to all nations, according to the commandment of the everlasting God, for obedience to the faith" (Rom. 16:26)

Indeed, the early church had no New Testament as we do. They studied the Old Testament under the apostles, whose teachings eventually became part of the Bible we have today. The Old Testament didn't become irrelevant after Jesus came; it became more relevant because God spoke about His plan far in advance through the patriarchs, the Law, and the prophets. Everything in the Bible, from Genesis to Revelation, is interconnected. Everything is mutually supporting, from the first word to the last amen. None is by happenstance, and God speaks through all of it.

Since the Old Testament contains types and shadows of New Testament realities, we can profitably look for prophetic, symbolic representations of all three baptisms. Let's touch on several examples. (Types and shadows biblically are representations of a specific truth that Jesus will eventually fulfill through His life, death, or resurrection.)

Paul writes, "Moreover, brethren, I do not want you to be unaware that all our fathers were under the cloud, all passed through the sea, all were baptized into Moses in the cloud and in the sea" (1 Cor. 10:1–2). Notice the three things into which they were baptized:

- Moses
- the cloud
- the sea

What do these represent? Moses was a type of Jesus. Moses' name means deliverer. He represented salvation from "Egypt," our old life in the world. The people of Israel were "saved" from Egypt before they even crossed the Red Sea. They left behind the shame and dishonor of their enslavement. They left behind their old identity as powerless victims in society. They experienced this deliverance by the blood of the lamb in the last judgment of Egypt. On that night, called the Passover in the Jewish faith, the spirit of death passed over Jewish households because they smeared the blood of an unblemished lamb on their doorposts. What an amazing picture of salvation!

The second baptism is pretty obvious. Paul says they passed through the sea, which represents water baptism. Through salvation, each of us came out of our own personal Egypt. Once we are free from slavery to darkness, the enemy always tries to convince us to return to our old life. He doesn't want us to progress to the second and third baptisms. He doesn't want us to publicly declare that we identify with Christ.

The sea is figuratively where our old man dies for good. For the people of Israel, this was an actual, physical reality of the Red Sea crashing in on the Egyptian army and killing them. The waters washed away the old things, representing the power of one's former life to enslave. That's what happens when we are born again and water baptized. We are set free—first in fact and then in practice as we walk it out among other believers. Water baptism helps to strip the enemy of his power to control by the greater power of our public declaration and identification with Christ.

Paul then mentions baptism into "the cloud." The Book of Exodus tells us that a cloud led the Israelites during the day, and a fire led them at night. This hovering, guiding, protective presence represents the Holy Spirit. He was with them through the wilderness in the form of cloud and fire. He leads us to the right place at the right time. He shields us from the scorching heat, provides warmth at night, and is a comforting presence we can look to anytime.

Once you see these marvelous symbols of the three baptisms in the Old Testament, you'll rejoice every time you come across them. They speak profoundly to our personal experience of the three baptisms today.

Here's one more example of many. God says these words to the nation of Israel: "Then I washed you in water; yes, I thoroughly washed off your blood, and I anointed you with oil" (Ezek. 16:9). In that brief passage, we see all three baptisms prophetically. Speaking through Ezekiel, God let us know that in the future we will be:

- washed in water—water baptism,
- thoroughly washed of blood—baptism into salvation, and
- anointed with oil—baptized in the Holy Spirit.

There are many such instances in the Old Testament, and I encourage you to watch for them as you read the Bible. God foretold the three baptisms His people should experience. It's not a new, strange doctrine but part of His eternal plan.

Three Baptisms in the Early Church

Because the Bible is consistent and interconnected, we also see the three baptisms throughout the New Testament. For example, on the day of Pentecost, when one hundred and twenty disciples received the baptism with the Holy Spirit in Jerusalem, Peter stood up and preached powerfully by the Holy Spirit. At the end of his message, the account reads:

> Now when they heard this, they were cut to the heart, and said to Peter and the rest of the apostles, "Men and brethren, what shall we do?"
>
> Then Peter said to them, "Repent, and let every one of you be baptized in the name of Jesus Christ for the remission of sins; and you shall receive the gift of the Holy Spirit. For the promise is to you and to your children, and to all who are afar off, as many as the Lord our God will call."
>
> —Acts 2:37–39

The three baptisms jump out at us: "repent," which is baptism into salvation; "be baptized in the name of Jesus Christ," which is water baptism; and "receive the gift of the Holy Spirit." Peter said the promise of the baptism in the Holy Spirit included those who are "afar off, as many as the Lord will call." That promise stretches through time and space to encompass every believer at all times—including you and me! We are invited and encouraged to experience all three baptisms as Peter preached on the church's birthday some two thousand years ago.

Just as Jesus' ministry only began after He was baptized in the Holy Spirit, the church's ministry only began after believers were baptized in the Holy Spirit.

Only then did the New Testament church start growing. In fact, the growth far exceeded normal human expectations. Three thousand were added in one day, an increase of twenty-five times! Just a few days later, it grew by another five thousand people. This was a staggering acceleration for a small, ragtag group of a few hundred people.

When persecution began, it pushed these believers beyond their boundaries, leading us to another example of the three baptisms. It's so exciting to see the Holy Spirit move in the scriptures.

Samaritans Baptized in the Holy Spirit

Eight years after one hundred and twenty radicals received the Holy Spirit on the day of Pentecost, Christians began to go into neighboring cities and areas to share the gospel, largely because of the persecution that broke out against them in Jerusalem. One disciple named Philip started preaching in Samaria, which was unusual and bold because Jews and Samaritans did not get along (that's a whole story in itself). They avoided each other as much as possible. Philip might have faced a hostile reception in bringing this new gospel, but he went anyway, obviously *under the influence* of the Holy Spirit.

According to Acts 8:12, two things happened when he preached: "they believed," which refers to the baptism into salvation; and "both men and women were baptized," which means being baptized in water. Then the account tells us:

> Now when the apostles who were at Jerusalem heard that Samaria had received the word of God, they sent Peter and John to them, who, when they had come down, prayed for them that they might receive the Holy Spirit. For as yet He had fallen upon none of them. They had only been baptized in the name of the Lord Jesus. Then they laid hands on them, and they received the Holy Spirit.
>
> —Acts 8:14–17

What a remarkable passage. It tells us that the disciples taught and practiced all three baptisms wherever they went. They established no Christian community without the practice of baptism into salvation, water baptism, and baptism with the Holy Spirit. And when the leading disciples in Jerusalem heard about the revival of salvation and water baptism that had broken out in Samaria, they went there to ensure the new Samaritan believers were receiving the third baptism.

Our pattern and practice today must be the same.

Gentiles Receive the Three Baptisms

Some Christians today say, "The baptism in the Holy Spirit may be for others, but it's not for me." The apostles made the same limiting distinction until God dramatically showed them that salvation, water baptism, and baptism with the Holy Spirit are for all people, not a select few.

One day, God told Peter to visit the house of a Roman centurion named Cornelius. Peter went to Cornelius' house and preached to his household and friends, whom Cornelius had called together for this very special and, it turns out, historic meeting:

> Then Peter opened his mouth and said: "In truth I perceive that God shows no partiality. But in every nation whoever fears Him and works righteousness is accepted by Him. The word which God sent to the children of Israel, preaching peace through Jesus Christ—He is Lord of all—that word you know, which was proclaimed throughout all Judea, and began from Galilee after the baptism which John preached: how God anointed Jesus of Nazareth with the Holy Spirit and with power, who went about doing good and healing all who were oppressed by the devil, for God was with Him.
>
> —Acts 10:34–38

Already, Peter spoke of the three baptisms in the believer's life. Then it says:

> While Peter was still speaking these words, the Holy Spirit fell upon all those who heard the word. And those of the circumcision who believed were astonished, as many as came with Peter, because the gift of the Holy Spirit had been poured out on the Gentiles also. For they heard them speak with tongues and magnify God. Then Peter answered, "Can anyone forbid water, that these should not be baptized who have received the Holy Spirit just as we have?" And he commanded them to be baptized in the name of the Lord.
>
> —Acts 10:44–48

This event was the first time non-Jews (Gentiles) had received the gospel and the baptism with the Holy Spirit, and it shocked Peter and his companions. In fact, when the other disciples in Jerusalem heard about it, they were skeptical and demanded that Peter come and explain himself!

This is a great example for us. Maybe we have, at some point in life, defined the third baptism outside the realm of our experience. But this account, among others, makes clear that all three baptisms are for all people at all times. That means you and me!

The Three Baptisms Go Global

My favorite example appears in Acts 19 when Paul traveled to minister for the first time in what was then called Asia and is now the country of Turkey. Ephesus was the capital city of biblical Asia. Here's what happened when Paul arrived there:

> And finding some disciples he said to them, "Did you receive the Holy Spirit when you believed?"
>
> So they said to him, "We have not so much as heard whether there is a Holy Spirit."
>
> And he said to them, "Into what then were you baptized?"
>
> So they said, "Into John's baptism."
>
> Then Paul said, "John indeed baptized with a baptism of repentance, saying to the people that they should believe on Him who would come after him, that is, on Christ Jesus."
>
> When they heard this, they were baptized in the name of the Lord Jesus. And when Paul had laid hands on them, the Holy Spirit came upon them, and they spoke with tongues and prophesied. Now the men were about twelve in all.
>
> —ACTS 19:1–7

The first question Paul asked was not, "Are you in a life group? Did you go to church this week? Have you given your tithes?" No. The first question he asked was, "Did you receive the Holy Spirit when you believed?" This is a monumental witness to the absolute necessity of receiving the baptism with the Holy Spirit. Paul recognized these men as believers because he referenced "when you believed." They were Christians who had not received the third baptism.

Many Christians find themselves in this situation

now. They believed the gospel and were baptized in water—but they don't understand and haven't received the third baptism. The best way out of a powerless life is to do what these men did. They responded, "We have not so much as heard whether there is a Holy Spirit."

I know I was like these men, having grown up in churches that didn't teach about a subsequent baptism with the Holy Spirit. I was joyful when I found out that night that there was a third baptism that empowered me in exciting new ways. I thought, "Why didn't anyone tell me about this before? This is great!"

If anyone has yet to receive the third baptism, it is not to their shame but to their joy because there is a great gift Jesus wants to give them. He wants to bring them completely under the influence of the promised Holy Spirit. When these dozen guys received the baptism in the Holy Spirit, it marked the beginning of the Ephesian church. The city of Ephesus and the province of Asia experienced what is certainly the greatest revival depicted in the New Testament and possibly in the entire Bible. The whole world changed—partly because these humble Christians discovered and received the baptism with the Holy Spirit.

You may wonder why these examples are in the Book of Acts and not in the Gospels. The answer is that the Holy Spirit could only "remain" on a saved person. Salvation was available after the death and resurrection of Jesus.

We also see numerous references to the three baptisms in the New Testament letters. For example:

- "The grace of the Lord Jesus Christ, and the love of God, and the communion of the Holy Spirit be with you all" (2 Cor. 13:14).

- "According to the foreknowledge of God the Father, in sanctification of the Spirit, for obedience and sprinkling of the blood of Jesus Christ" (1 Pet. 1:2).

- "For there are three that bear witness in heaven: the Father, the Word, and the Holy Spirit; and these three are one" (1 John 5:7–8).

References to threes abound in the Bible. But even with a firm biblical foundation for the third baptism, some believers shy away from the experience. Let's take a look at some common reasons why.

Father, as I continue to read and meditate over the above scriptures and stories, open my eyes to the baptism with the Holy Spirit. Even as I read the Bible, help me see things I have not seen. I pray that the influence of the Holy Spirit will be real and change me. In Jesus' name, amen.

Reflections for Further Study

1. How does it inform your view of God's work through the Holy Spirit that the three baptisms have been present or foreshadowed from the beginning?

2. Explain in your own words why you think God does things in threes.

3. The early disciples preached and implemented the three baptisms wherever they went. Reflect on why they did this and its effects on those who became disciples of Jesus in their day.

4. Paul ended his second letter to the Corinthian church with these words:

   > The grace of the Lord Jesus Christ, and the love of God, and the communion of the Holy Spirit be with you all. Amen.
   >
   > —2 Corinthians 13:14

   Consider the three aspects of relationship attributed to the three members of the godhead (grace, love, and communion). How does this simple farewell illuminate the roles of the Father, Son, and Holy Spirit in our lives?

CHAPTER 5

BARRIERS TO RECEIVING THE HOLY SPIRIT

THIS TOPIC OF baptism in the Holy Spirit makes some people uncomfortable. They think that when people are under the influence of the Holy Spirit, everyone will start acting weird. Someone will jump over the pews and run around the church, someone else will start prophesying in a loud voice, and others will lay hands on and pray for everyone they can find, demanding that they speak in tongues. Or something crazy and out of control will happen in the middle of Walmart—well, even more crazy than what already happens in a Walmart. Many people have had negative or confusing experiences because of how the ministry and baptism in the Holy Spirit are sometimes presented or taught. Understandably, they push away this biblical experience given to empower them. But they lose the infinite benefit of having an effective partner in everyday life.

People recoil from this third baptism because of the instinctive human fear of anything supernatural. By this, I mean that people are afraid anytime something supernatural happens, even if it's positive. The main reason is that we often have difficulty explaining or understanding it. Hopefully, this book helps in clearing up some of these questions. But often, we have to receive things by faith without fully understanding them. The Bible clearly shows this. Consider how many times Jesus performed a miracle and, in response, people were afraid. For example:

- When Jesus healed a paralytic in front of a crowd of people, "they were all amazed, and they glorified God and were filled with fear, saying, 'We have seen strange things today!'" (Luke 5:26).

- When Jesus raised a widow's son from the dead, "Then fear came upon all" (Luke 7:16).

- When Jesus cast a legion of demons out of a crazed man and restored him to his right mind, the people from that area came to investigate, and "they were afraid" (Luke 8:35).

- On the Sea of Galilee, Jesus calmed a storm, and His disciples "were afraid" (Luke 8:25).

- When Jesus caused some of His disciples to catch a miraculously large amount of fish, Peter fell at His feet, and Jesus had to tell him, "Do not be afraid" (Luke 5:10).

Whenever an angel of the Lord came to someone in the Old and New Testaments, people invariably fell down, overcome by fear. The angels were always commanding them, "Do not be afraid."

Why are people afraid of miracles, healings, and heavenly visitations? Because they are so foreign to our minds and senses. We aren't accustomed to supernatural occurrences. It's beyond our realm of comfort and understanding. We don't know how to rationalize or process what's happening. We feel vulnerable, confused, and sometimes overwhelmed—even when God is doing something good! The supernatural is spiritual, not natural.

This is also true of the baptism with the Holy Spirit. It is, by definition, a supernatural experience. It can happen in near-silence or be joyous and noisy, but one thing is sure: it is a spiritual reality breaking into a person's life. That is what makes it so powerful, beyond anything earthly. I like to say it's a little bit of heaven coming to earth.

If your hesitation about the third baptism and the influence of the Holy Spirit is fear, I encourage you to obey the words of Jesus and the angels throughout the Bible: "Do not be afraid." Don't let fear keep you from the powerful, positive lifestyle of walking in the Holy Spirit. If you think about it, everything is freaky until you get used to it: marriage, a new job, driving a different car, living in a new neighborhood or city. We still do these things because they are good. We should not reject an experience with the Holy Spirit because it seems scary or makes us uncomfortable. Overcoming that fear is just part of living.

The baptism with the Holy Spirit is your right as a believer and your gift from above. We all need it.

> *Lord, I ask You to remove any fear of the Holy Spirit or the supernatural. I know that You have not given me a spirit of fear. God, You have given me a spirit of peace. I receive freedom from fear now in Jesus' name.*

It Doesn't Have to Be Weird

As I mentioned, others find the subject of Holy Spirit baptism distasteful because of how some ministers, ministries, and television preachers have presented it. This is unfortunate. If the devil can convince people (as he often does) that the baptism with the Holy Spirit is weird, he can scare them away from one of the most empowering things that could ever happen to them. One way he accomplishes this is by convincing some ministers or people to do odd things in the name of the "Holy Spirit." This sends well-meaning, receptive people heading for the exits—nobody can blame them. Nobody wants to experience weirdness.

I don't consider myself weird, and I'm not too fond of weird things. I'm a level-headed, logical thinker who enjoys mathematics and excels at finances and investing. I avoid strange people and meetings or ministries that feel "off." I can testify that in thirty-plus years since I was baptized in the Holy Spirit, I have not found the experience, or the Holy Spirit Himself, to be weird, nor does He cause me to do, think, or say strange things under his influence. My relationship with Him is supernatural without being bizarre. I think this is what He wants for you, too. Are there some things that take time to understand? Absolutely. That is the place that I must use my faith and trust Scripture.

I had one experience early on in my Christian life that profoundly impacted me and was, at least by my definition, very unusual. I want to share that as a way of being honest while also showing that, while God infrequently does unusual supernatural things in the life of a believer, the baptism with the Holy Spirit is mainly a day-to-day walk that looks rather normal. I have only told this experience to a dozen or so people up to now, so here goes.

My Crazy Experience With God

It was February 1996. I was twenty-seven years old and had been a Christian for about six years. At that moment in my life, I was wrestling with God over the direction of my life. I knew that God wanted me to do something significant beyond attending church and serving as a volunteer minister. I couldn't see the path ahead clearly. So when I heard that a minister who functioned powerfully in the Holy Spirit was coming to our church for a series of services, I took the entire week off work to attend the meetings.

The minister was well-known, and I had heard a lot about him. They scheduled him to preach three times every day all week long. I attended every meeting, and every time, he preached a different message to packed rooms and a big auditorium. It was amazing to watch, and because I was serving as a pastor's aide, I sat on the front row and assisted with whatever was happening. Sometimes this meant getting something for the pastor; other times, it meant helping with ministry moments in the services. I also spent a lot of time praying over others, receiving prayer myself, and enjoying the presence of God. It was a powerful week.

On the last night, Saturday, the pastor went to the platform and said, "I want to share a video of an event that happened in Florida where a church was worshiping spontaneously, and you could hear angels singing." He showed the video on our church's big screen, and it was awesome to watch (and hear) what had happened. As a result, the people in our sanctuary went into a time of worship and adoration of God. I was on the front row, sitting right next to our pastor, who was worshiping.

In the middle of that magnificent moment, the Lord told me, "Get up and walk to the front."

"Oh, no," I thought. "There's no way I should do that right now."

God didn't say anything more or repeat the command. He knew I had heard it.

I sighed, humbled myself, and obeyed, walking to the altar area alone. Nobody followed me, and nobody said anything to me. I was the head pastor's assistant, and they probably assumed I had something to do there. Having done what God told me to do, I sat back down.

God gave me another command: "Do it again, but this time do a three-hundred-sixty-degree spin."

"That's crazy," I thought bluntly. "I'm not doing that. I do not get caught up and do things like that." This whole conversation was happening in my head. I was kind of arguing with God.

Again, God didn't repeat it, but the command hung over me. Groaning inwardly, I went forward and did a three-hundred-sixty-degree turn very grudgingly. It didn't feel significant or helpful to anyone at all. I went and sat back down, and things got even stranger because suddenly, I couldn't move. I couldn't stand up. It was like I'd gone into a trance but was still aware of my surroundings. It was like a heavy blanket was lowered over me. The service continued for a while, then concluded—and still, the presence of the Holy Spirit rested on me so strongly that I could not move. People left me alone, knowing something was happening to me. Eventually, everyone left the auditorium, and I was alone—and still, I could not move.

Finally, after about an hour, I could stand up and walk to the bathroom. As soon as I walked in, the presence of God came on me, and I started weeping like never before. It felt like somebody had plugged me into an electrical socket. I was thankful it was only me in there. Surging power overcame me, stopped for a moment, and hit me again with great force. I had never felt anything like it and found it hard to stand up, so I fell to my knees and then onto my face, right on the bathroom floor.

The power went away a third time, then hit me again. I didn't know what to expect next, but what happened was beyond extraordinary and had never happened to me before or since. As God is my witness, Jesus walked into the bathroom. I couldn't see His face or make out the color of His eyes or anything, but He was there. I was laying on my face, weeping all the while. Jesus came over, touched my hands and mouth, and then left. The presence of God lifted, and I sat up, shocked at what had just occurred.

What just happened to me? I wondered, unable to even categorize it in any rational way. I stood up, washed my face, and walked to my car. The parking lot was virtually empty. Snow covered the ground in Richmond, and I drove home through a whitened landscape. As soon as I walked in our front door, the power of God overwhelmed Penny, and she started weeping without any warning or build-up.

The next morning was Sunday, and we attended morning services at the church. Again, I was in the front row worshiping God, and suddenly, I witnessed a vision of the night before. It was as if a movie screen popped in front of me with my eyes wide open. I saw myself sitting in the front row and then standing and walking to the front, as I had done. A door had opened in the corner of the room, floor-to-ceiling tall. Then I saw myself sitting back down.

I watched myself walk forward again in the vision and do the full-circle turn. But now I could see that as I obeyed God, angels filed onto the platform from a side door and lined the auditorium's walls. They were so tall that their heads went above the ceiling; all I could see were their bodies. After a while, they filed back out the door through which they'd come. Then the vision ended.

This experience awed and unsettled me. It was mostly disruptive at the time, not the heavenly interruption I was looking for. As I reflected on it, I had a strong sense that my goal of becoming successful in business and funding churches and ministries through wealth would not happen. Rather, it seemed God had a different direction for me, but I didn't know what it was.

As time went on, I began to understand that I had been so hungry for God's presence and direction that He graciously came and, in an unusual way, communicated, "You're my kid, and I'm going to use you. I will not tell you how, but I will use you." Among other things, the experience showed me that our hunger level determines our level of experiencing God. Jesus' words became a reality for me: "Hunger and thirst for righteousness, and you will be filled" (See Matthew 5:6.) Without knowing it, I was very hungry for leadership and affirmation from God at that time.

I also saw, over time, that while I thought I had God and the world all figured out, I had no idea about either. The unusual experience prompted me to rely on the influence of the Holy Spirit much more in everyday life. There was a lot I didn't know—but He knew everything, and He would guide me faithfully.

Today, I see the experience as marking the beginning of my ministry. At that moment, God called me and assured me that He would use me for future work. Six years later, Penny and I moved to a city we knew little about and planted a church that has flourished under the Holy Spirit's leadership and our humble obedience. Through all the various battles, hurdles, and victories, I look back at that strange experience as a watershed moment in my life.

Timothy in the Bible had something similar happen to him. Paul wrote to him once to say, in essence, "Remember that time I laid hands on you? Don't forget that. Stir that memory up. Reflect on it and let it energize you anew." Then he told Timothy not to be afraid but to stand in the present power of that experience, boldly ministering in his day. Paul was referring to a supernatural touchstone moment Timothy could draw from.

Would I accept another experience like that? Sure, gladly, but I'm not necessarily looking for one. My point in sharing it is that God does not give visions or visitations like that every day. It's not how He runs things in our lives—at least not in mine nor in the lives of the thousands of people I've ministered with and know. God will meet us at critical times if He knows we need that kind of experience, and those are amazing. But the more mature we get, the less those touchstone encounters seem to happen. It's not that He leaves us alone; it's that we have the faith to know He's there even without a vision or an immediate, in-person encounter. Faith pleases Him, and He calls us to walk by faith, not sight. We're also called to walk by faith, not feelings. Faith is always a choice and may or may not have feelings with it.

Walking under the influence of the Holy Spirit is a daily miracle, and I believe God enjoys the relational aspect of this more than the spectacular effect of unusual supernatural experiences. In other words, walking with the Holy Spirit is more supernaturally normal than most people guess.

Some people spend so much time looking for a word or supernatural experience that it's as if they want to walk by sight, not faith. That's not how this life works. As I grow in my relationship with the Holy Spirit, I don't get as many messages from God through people inspired by the Holy Spirit. In other words, I don't get a lot of direction outside of my daily time with God. I think it's because I talk to Him a lot already. The moment I start getting words from other people, it usually means I'm not listening to Him myself. Other times it means He's confirming something important for me.

There is a great example of this in 1 Kings 19. I would like to paraphrase this moment that the prophet Elijah has with God. We can call this the Maxwell translation. Elijah had just done some incredibly miraculous things. He defeated 850 false prophets, called fire down from heaven, and ran faster than the king's chariot. Then he prayed for rain in a drought, and it rained. Now Elijah has hit a low point. He has seen all the spectacular and he needs direction from God. He finds himself in a cave, looking for God and wanting to find Him in the spectacular. The Bible tells us that the earth shakes, the wind blows, and fire comes. But God is not in any of these spectacular things. Lastly, there is a still, small voice. The scripture says, God is in the "still small voice" (1 Kings 19:12). It's not the spectacular but the quiet, normal voice of God.

Often, this is how the Holy Spirit will influence our lives. It happens in the simple, everyday time with God. You can always listen because He is always there.

The Holy Spirit doesn't invite us to a life of weirdness but to a daily experience of Him, which is mostly one-on-one and relational.

People Want Supernatural Reality

I see more people having a desire for spiritual things than ever before. They want to know what walking with God looks like and feels like. They want to understand who the Holy Spirit is, how He is involved in our everyday lives, and what it means to be baptized in the Holy Spirit, live under His influence, and minister in supernatural power as He created us to do.

Many different teachings sweep through churches—on leadership, church growth, small groups, discipleship, outreach, worship, and so on—and all these emphases have their place, but the underlying thing people crave is spiritual. It's what they mean when they say they want authenticity.

They want to experience God and see miracles for themselves, even if it's a little scary or confusing. They want the trustworthy leadership of the Holy Spirit to become a reality in their lives, churches, and families. They want people who have an experiential understanding of this third baptism to lead them into a relationship with the Holy Spirit.

This subject is not going away. Rather, hunger is growing worldwide. I believe this is what the church needs. I believe that this relationship with the Holy Spirit is what will change our communities, families, and country. We need an outpouring of God's Spirit, the Holy Spirit, in our lives. And it starts in each one of us.

What should you do if you've been burned by a church

or minister purportedly exercising the gifts or power of the Holy Spirit but seeming to get into some weirdness? First, don't let it separate you from the faithful Father God is and the wonderful gift God has for you. We've all had a bad experience at a restaurant, but none of us quit going to restaurants. Nothing and nobody should have the power to cut you off from a blessing God prepared for you before the foundation of the world. It is yours by divine inheritance. It was foretold throughout Scripture and promised to you personally and specifically in multiple places in the Bible. The third baptism is too valuable for you to let someone steal it from you through a bad example.

Second, evaluate what happened based on the Word of God. Take the opportunity to study through the negative experience. Dive into what the Word says about the ministry of the Holy Spirit. Talk to Him about what happened. He will give you insight.

Third, look at the fruit of all ministries and ministers. Does the ministry result in love, joy, peace, patience, and the other characteristics of the Spirit? Does the life of the minister reflect the character of Christ? Who gets the attention from what happens—a person or Jesus?

Those are a few easy ways to walk through what happened to you and clear away the rubble of disappointment, anger, or whatever hinders you from moving ahead and living under the influence of the Holy Spirit. *Finally, let me assure you that the Holy Spirit is not weird, but people certainly can be!* The truth is that people who act weird after being baptized in the Holy Spirit were usually weird before they were baptized in the Holy Spirit. The baptism in the Holy Spirit does not cure weirdness. Just because a person is weird, that doesn't make Him weird. They may go on being weird after being baptized in the Holy Spirit, but it doesn't bother the Lord. He has a plan and a future for that person, just as He does for you and me.

Let nothing stand in your way of receiving this magnificent gift—not fear of the supernatural, not fear of becoming weird or enduring weirdness. The Holy Spirit is waiting to help you in every area of life—your marriage, your job, your finances, your parenting, your career, your ministry, and much more. Let's examine how baptism with the Holy Spirit will powerfully improve your life experience.

Reflections for Further Study

1. What are your biggest barriers to receiving the baptism in the Holy Spirit or some other work of the Holy Spirit?

2. Have you witnessed negative or off-putting behavior that was attributed to the Holy Spirit? Talk about what happened.

3. Have you ever experienced the Holy Spirit in an unusual or unexpected way? Explain.

4. Do you observe hunger for the supernatural in other people's lives—and your own? Describe what that looks like.

5. Read and consider Paul's words about the work of the Holy Spirit in church life.

> But the manifestation of the Spirit is given to each one for the profit of all: for to one is given the word of wisdom through the Spirit, to another the word of knowledge through the same Spirit, to another faith by the same Spirit, to another gifts of healings by the same Spirit, to another the working of miracles, to another prophecy, to another discerning of spirits, to another different kinds of tongues, to another the interpretation of tongues.

> But one and the same Spirit works all these things, distributing to each one individually as He wills.
>
> For as the body is one and has many members, but all the members of that one body, being many, are one body, so also *is* Christ. For by one Spirit we were all baptized into one body—whether Jews or Greeks, whether slaves or free—and have all been made to drink into one Spirit.
>
> —1 Corinthians 12:7–13

6. Have you seen spiritual gifts operate in a healthy way in a church or group of believers? What did that look like?

CHAPTER 6

WHAT DOES THE HOLY SPIRIT DO?

NOT LONG AFTER Penny and I married, we purchased a brand-new queen-size bed. We needed it. I had slept on a waterbed as a single guy, and she wasn't about to have that thing in the house any longer than needed. She wanted a four-poster, which I learned is a bed with four posts. You can tell I'm a quick learner. Maybe some of you know that, but it was a new concept to me. So we went shopping and bought a whole bedroom suite to replace our mismatched stuff and that crazy waterbed. This new suite came with a chest of drawers, side tables, and a beautiful new mattress. Penny was excited, and I was excited. Our home was coming together brilliantly.

As we were driving home from buying these things, Penny told me, "Now we need to get a new comforter." That sounded great to me. I love crawling under the covers with a new set of clean sheets. I love my pillow. I love the whole experience of going to bed, and a new comforter would only make it better.

So Penny went comforter shopping, which took more time than I expected, and one day she called me from the store.

"I found the right one," she said.

"Awesome. How much is it?" I asked.

When she told me, I about fell off my chair at work. I didn't know a decent comforter would require a second mortgage. But after recovering from sticker shock and agreeing to the purchase, I started looking forward to getting home and going to bed. Penny told me how wonderful the comforter was, how we would feel like a king and queen in our new bedroom suite, and so on.

I walked into the house after work and could smell the rich mahogany of the new furniture. Penny and I enjoyed a great dinner together because Penny is an amazing cook. Then we watched a little television, but the whole time I was thinking, "I can't wait to get in the bed with that nice, plush comforter. I will pull it up to my chin, and we can snuggle and spoon underneath it. It's going to be so much fun."

After a while, bedtime finally arrived. Penny went into the bedroom first. I turned the lights off in the front rooms, locked the front door, and walked into our bedroom, expecting to see the comforter in all its glory sitting atop our bed. I was greeted instead by the sight of the brand-new, mortgage-level comforter folded neatly and placed on the floor to the side.

"What's going on?" I asked.

"With what?" Penny asked innocently.

"With the comforter," I said. "I've been looking forward to sleeping under it."

She walked toward me with that look that said, "Now, my dear husband, let me explain."

"Sweetheart," she told me, "the comforter is not for use but only for looks."

"What?" I thought. "I paid that much for a comforter I don't even get to use?"

My dreams of snuggling underneath it crashed to the floor.

And that's how it was. The amazing comforter never actually gave us warmth. Yes, we had great new sheets and blankets, but that expensive comforter never graced our bed while we were in it.

It wasn't the only time I learned that some furniture is never to be used. Marriage soon taught me that many of my possessions are just for looks. I am not allowed to enter whole rooms of our house unless someone comes over. We don't bring out certain towels unless guests are present. They can use them, but I can't. We even have chairs and tables that are not for use unless we have people at our house. An invisible boundary line keeps me away from those special pieces I own but never actually use unless we're hosting. The interesting thing about this experience is so many of my pastor friends have had the same experience. I recently read a book by Pastor Robert Morris, and he tells a similar story.

THE HOLY SPIRIT, YOUR FRIEND

That unused comforter became a perfect picture of how many Christians and churches treat the true Comforter, the Holy Spirit. They keep Him around for looks but never allow Him to do anything useful, either in their life or in their church. They live mostly outside of His influence. He is depicted in the stained glass and sung about in the songs, but He never becomes a living, personal friend and partner. Like the comforter on my bed, the Holy Spirit remains nice-looking but non-functioning in the lives of many believers.

Thank God it doesn't need to be that way. The Holy Spirit is not just for looks. He promises to comfort and talk with us in every circumstance, counsel us in the way we should go, lead us into truth, and walk alongside us every moment of the day as our companion. He is not a mist, a wind, a transparent ghostly figure, or a silent partner. He is God. He is a wonderful Person with whom we can and must have a vibrant and life-giving personal relationship.

Jesus described Him this way:

> I will talk to the Father, and he'll provide you another Friend so that you will always have someone with you. This Friend is the Spirit

> of Truth. The godless world can't take him in because it doesn't have eyes to see him, doesn't know what to look for. But you know him already because he has been staying with you, and will even be in you!
>
> —JOHN 14:16–17, MSG

I love how *The Message* Bible articulates those verses. The Holy Spirit is primarily your Friend, someone you can know and love. When people describe the Holy Spirit just in terms of how people respond to His presence—with a shout, goose bumps, a tingle up the neck, a tear—they miss the Person. These are all effects of His presence, but we should relate to Him as a Person, not merely as a power source or a heavenly vending machine. Like any friend, He doesn't want to be ignored, taken advantage of, or forgotten about. He wants to interact with each believer. He promises to listen, respond, and always act in our best interests.

He is always a positive, healthy influence and never a bad one.

Only when you have a vibrant relationship with Him personally will you appreciate all He does in your life. Only then will you experience His comprehensive comfort.

He Brings Order from Chaos

Some people think the influence of the Holy Spirit in their lives will mess everything up. They picture Him as unpredictable, confusing, or out of control. To them,

He is associated with wild church services, revival meetings, or a crazy television preacher.

In reality, the Holy Spirit does exactly the opposite. He organizes and uncomplicates our lives. He brings order out of any level of chaos. We know this because the first time He was mentioned in Scripture, He was hovering above a formless creation, preparing to bring order to it (Gen. 1:2). The law of first mention, a way to interpret things in the Bible, tells us this is the key to His nature. He takes messes and makes miracles. He turns problems into purpose. If your life feels chaotic and disorganized, you need the baptism in the Holy Spirit. If things seem tangled up, He's the one who can bring order out of your situation. In fact, the Holy Spirit does His best work when things are all jumbled up.

My wife has a very special gift. She can walk into a room or a large space anywhere and see what can become of it. She envisions the design and then carries it out. I mean if you see the before and after pictures of me, you can tell my wife is gifted. This is a picture of the Holy Spirit's influence. He can enter any circumstance and improve it, turning confusion into peace and disrepair into optimum performance.

But some people are so comfortable with chaos that they don't want it straightened out. The apostle John wrote that "men loved darkness" and rejected the Light of the world (John 3:19). I see that tendency in myself. Sometimes I ignore the Holy Spirit when He draws attention to a chaotic area of my life because I don't want to change it. It can feel like He's getting into my personal space and pointing out stuff I don't want to see. Yes, we all have areas that need to be reordered or even removed, but it can feel like an invasion when the Holy Spirit accepts our invitation and gets involved.

But in the end His heavenly ordering always brings relief.

In 2001 God spoke to Penny and me—we were married and had children by then—to move from our native Richmond, Virginia, and plant a church in Charlotte, North Carolina. We knew nothing about Charlotte and had never planted a church before, but we felt peace about it. So we moved to Charlotte and got ready for what was next.

Around that time, we received a call from Pastor Dennis Rouse, who had preached the night I was saved and baptized in the Holy Spirit. He had since moved to Atlanta to plant Victory World Church. He asked us to come to spend the weekend in Atlanta with him. We took our three young kids and showed up in our maroon Volvo with 230,000 miles on it, leaking oil everywhere.

Dennis was beyond gracious. "What are you going to do in Charlotte?" he asked us at one point while we were catching up.

"Plant a church," we said by faith, without even knowing what that looked like.

To our surprise, on Sunday morning, Pastor Dennis called us up on the platform of his church and gave us $10,000 toward the founding of Freedom House Church. That was a major confirmation that we had heard and were obeying the helper in our move and ministry. It also brought necessary structure and planning to our efforts.

Remember that the Holy Spirit is drawn to situations that need help. He likes unlikely and intimidating situations because He sees all the possibilities that can come from influencing them. It's our job to invite His influence into those circumstances because our lives remain disordered without Him. His eternal role is to bring harmony and structure to families, churches, societies, and more, just as He did from our beginning with Freedom House. He helps us find the right pathway to walk down. We cannot do any of this on our own. Our daily prayer should be, "Holy Spirit, please bring greater order to my life. Take over any areas of chaos. I surrender them to You, and I know You will make things work well for me."

Having walked this way for more than thirty years, I don't know how anyone lives without the help of the Holy Spirit in bringing order to their lives. Without Him, I would be a mess.

Let's look at other ways He carries out this primary mission.

HE IS YOUR HELPER

Mark Twain, one of the great authors of the nineteenth century, wrote a book in 1883 called *Life on the Mississippi.* In it, he described his time as a Mississippi steamboat pilot. The mighty Mississippi River is the fourth-longest in the world and is uniquely crooked, making it extremely difficult to navigate. If you wanted to traverse it without damaging the boat or cargo, your best bet was to hire a riverboat captain, as Twain described. Interestingly, the riverboat captain would come aboard but not take the boat's wheel. Rather, he stood behind the pilot (the one driving the boat) and guided him up, down, and around the river according to the nuances he was familiar with. The riverboat captain knew where the water was shallow and where it was deep. He knew when the pilot needed to turn right or left to avoid an underground obstacle or to catch a helpful current and how to get through the most tortuous and challenging sections without trouble.

That is a great picture of what the Holy Spirit does. He doesn't grab the wheel of our lives. He comes alongside us and influences and guides us through the crooked passages. He says, "Don't go over there because it's too shallow, and the boat might run aground. Make sure you turn here a little bit to avoid that sandbar. Now come here and catch this current. You'll get where you're going a lot faster." This is the essence of supernatural living. It is most often subtle and internal, not flashy and external. The Holy Spirit is our riverboat captain on life's otherwise treacherous and unpredictable journey.

Jesus said it this way the night before He was crucified: "If you love Me, keep My commandments. And I will pray the Father, and He will give you another Helper, that He may abide with you forever—the Spirit of truth" (John 14:15–17).

You can see in Jesus' description that the Holy Spirit

will never lead you into error or deception but only into truth. The world moves ahead in darkness and deception, never really knowing the truth in a certain situation, but the guidance of the Holy Spirit allows you to see things clearly. Every morning you can wake up and invite the Holy Spirit to show you the truth about the day to come. When a tough decision confronts you, you tune your heart to hear what the Holy Spirit says about it. When a friend comes to you in a bad situation needing immediate advice, you're already walking in truth and can ask the Holy Spirit for wisdom and counsel.

Maybe the most important habit you can get into is to invite the Holy Spirit into every conversation and situation you enter. Before making a business decision, ask Him to help you. Sometimes He has someone for you to talk to, or He wants to help you avoid bad traffic or something worse. He is such a great Friend.

When you walk into the house after a long day, and things are a mess—the kids are running around like banshees, and your spouse is seemingly sitting there doing nothing but looking at an iPhone—ask for the Holy Spirit's perspective on what's happening before you launch into blame. He knows what kind of day your spouse had, and you don't. Listen to your Guide, and He will lead you to do and say the right things—rather than nuking things with ill-advised words.

Most of our interactions and experiences with the Holy Spirit happen internally, in our thought lives, but they are reflected and carried out in public view. A person under the Holy Spirit's influence goes through life confident and peaceful instead of random, run-down, and raggedy.

He Teaches You

Jesus also said, "The helper, the Holy Spirit, whom the Father will send in my name, will teach you all things." God is the supreme expert in everything. Why wouldn't we ask Him about everything in our lives? We have the option of being His students. When we invite Him to, He will teach us all things.

To be taught is to retain a lesson for future use. It's like the pilot of a boat in our previous example. After a few trips up and down the river, he learns how to navigate it. As the Holy Spirit builds knowledge and wisdom into us, He encourages us to draw on it to make the right decisions. He doesn't just want to stand behind us and guide us; He wants us to resemble Him in our thinking and our exercise of knowledge.

It starts with our humbly becoming His students every day. I do it this way: Before everything I do, I ask Him to teach me through it. I place myself directly under His influence. When I open my Bible to read, I invite the Holy Spirit to unlock lessons for me. When I worship, I invite Him to guide my heart to sing and do what pleases the Father. In all these circumstances, you will find something that stands out to you—a word or phrase in the Bible, a lyric of a song, or something someone says in a conversation. The Holy Spirit highlights what you should pay attention to—and teaches you about those things.

He Testifies Through You

The church I was saved in emphasized the powerful working of the Holy Spirit when a group of believers gathers, and I believe in that. But when I began studying the ministry of the Holy Spirit by reading the Bible, I was surprised to find that one of His main functions is to testify of Jesus. (To testify means to share how God's story has influenced your story.)

In Jesus' last words on earth, He tells us this is something the Holy Spirit will do: "But you shall receive power when the Holy Spirit has come upon you; and you shall be witnesses to Me in Jerusalem, and in all Judea and Samaria, and to the end of the earth" (Acts 1:8).

I had seen the Holy Spirit do amazing things in church services and other ministry venues. I had seen His power evidenced when people laid hands on the sick to heal them, spoke in other tongues, and prophesied. All these things were real. But when I read Jesus' words before He ascended to heaven, I saw how important it is that the Holy Spirit gives us the power to testify.

The first principle I take out of this is that whenever the Holy Spirit is at work, in whatever environment and expression, He will always influence it toward Jesus. He will never highlight or exalt a person. He won't even make a miracle or demonstration of power the central focus. Rather, everything testifies to the power, character, and praiseworthiness of Jesus Himself.

Think about it: A witness testifies of what he has seen. There are no secondary witnesses. So in what way are Christians today witnesses of Jesus? Nobody alive today was present at the resurrection. None of us saw firsthand the ministry of Jesus or heard His teaching—nobody, that is, except the Holy Spirit. This is why it is His job to testify through us. I didn't see Jesus rise from the dead—but the Holy Spirit did. I didn't hear the Sermon on the Mount—but the Holy Spirit did. When we teach and share the gospel, the Holy Spirit affirms it powerfully in the hearts and minds of listeners, just as He did through the Book of Acts when Peter and others preached as witnesses of the risen Christ.

The Holy Spirit also does this eternally in heaven, revealing the Father. In Isaiah 6, God takes the prophet into the spirit and the presence of God and the seraphim ("burning ones"), a type of angel and angels who cry, "Holy, holy, holy!" around the throne for eternity.

I used to wonder why they kept saying the same thing, and then it occurred to me. Every time they finish, the Holy Spirit reveals a different aspect of the Father. Their view of Him shifts like diamonds, and new facets are visible. In response, the angels again cry, "Holy!" The Holy Spirit reveals God to us in all His facets. As Paul wrote, He searches "the deep things of God" (1 Cor. 2:10).

The Holy Spirit empowers us to provide a continuing witness of Jesus, who works through His people in word and action. Jesus said, "The works that I do in My

Father's name, they bear witness of Me" (John 10:25). The Holy Spirit gives us the power to testify of Him and to demonstrate His character, power, and will by doing the works Jesus did and commanded us to do.

Sometimes, those works take us directly into the realm of supernatural confrontation, as we will see in the next chapter.

Dear heavenly Father, I desire to have the Holy Spirit order my life. I need Him to remove all confusion and point me to the truth. I ask the Holy Spirit to help me be a better witness to the goodness of Jesus. In Jesus' name, amen.

Reflections for Further Study

1. Do you have a friendship with the Holy Spirit? How would you describe your relationship with Him?

2. Which areas of your life could use organizing? Which feel most chaotic? Write a few lines of prayer, inviting the Holy Spirit to help you in these areas.

3. In what ways have you been taught by the Holy Spirit, especially recently? Describe them here.

4. Do you consider yourself an effective witness of Jesus Christ? Why or why not?

5. Consider Jesus' words in the following passage:

    > I still have many things to say to you, but you cannot bear them now. However, when He, the Spirit of truth, has come, He will guide you into all truth; for He will not speak on His own authority, but whatever He hears He will speak; and He will tell you things to come. He will glorify Me, for He will take of what is Mine and declare it to you. All things that the

> Father has are Mine. Therefore I said that He will take of Mine and declare it to you.
>
> —John 16:12–15

6. In what way does the Holy Spirit guide you into all truth and "declare" the things of Jesus to you? To what extent is this a reality in your life? Explain.

CHAPTER 7

WHAT IS SPIRITUAL POWER?

I'VE HEARD THE story of Dwight Moody, the famous twentieth-century evangelist who had a very large church in Chicago, which was probably one of the first megachurches in the United States. It grew to a certain point and hit the ceiling. Over time two ladies, Mrs. Cook and Auntie Snow, began sitting on the front row every Sunday. They told Moody after a service one time, "Pastor, we've been praying for you, and we're not going to stop until you receive the baptism in the Holy Spirit."

Moody was a bit taken aback and thought, "What do you mean by the baptism of the Holy Spirit? Am I missing something in my walk with the Lord?" But he took it graciously, and the women continued to sit on the front row and tell him over the months, in a respectful way, "We are praying that you would receive the baptism in the Holy Spirit." His usual response was, "I would rather you pray for the church," but they told him, "The church will catch fire when you do."

One day Moody finally said to them, "Tell me more about this baptism in the Holy Spirit." And so they did. As a result, he began studying Acts 2 with an open mind and a new perspective on the third baptism. He prayed, "God, if this is something I should have, then I want it."

He was in New York getting ready to go to London to preach. While walking through New York's financial district, the Holy Spirit suddenly fell on him. Moody was overtaken and had to rush to a friend's house to experience what was happening. He spent four or five hours in a room, praying as God poured the Holy Spirit out on his life. At that moment, his entire ministry changed.

The next message he preached, hundreds, if not thousands, came to know Jesus as Lord and Savior. When Moody walked through factories and train stations, he didn't even need to say a word; people would fall on their knees and begin to repent of their sins. The baptism in the Holy Spirit elevated this great man's ministry to a new level of effectiveness. And the great news is this baptism is available for every believer.

All Problems Are Spiritual Problems

Every problem we face in life is a spiritual issue and must be dealt with spiritually. Think of the major events and victories of the Bible. Moses held up his hands, and God split the Red Sea. Samson, empowered by the Holy Spirit, killed a lion with his bare hands and took down a whole army with the jawbone of a donkey. David, just a teenager at the time, faced Goliath with a slingshot and defeated him.

One of my favorite men in the Bible, Elijah, showed up at one of the most difficult times in Israel's history. A crazy woman named Jezebel was pushing false worship and idols on the people. Her husband, King Ahab, was an ineffective pushover. Elijah called fire down from heaven and slayed four hundred false prophets. Not only that, but he outran the king's chariot for twenty-five miles!

Consider Jesus, who performed countless miracles through the power of the Holy Spirit. He walked on water, calmed storms, healed blind eyes and deaf ears, raised the dead, multiplied food, and much more. Acts 10:38 says, "God anointed Jesus of Nazareth with the Holy Spirit and with power, who went about doing good and healing all who were oppressed by the devil."

We may not engage in a major miracle ministry as Jesus did or confront leaders of nations as Elijah did, but we all have lives to live and battles to fight. Think of the antagonistic girl or guy at work who doesn't like Christians. Or the people in our kids' schools or on their sports teams who disagree with biblical truth. Or the family, neighbors, and church members who rub us the wrong way. Or what we are facing as a nation on marriage, gender, and identity. We have a lot to overcome, and we will only do it successfully if we are baptized in the Holy Spirit as Jesus was and living under the Holy Spirit's influence.

We need spiritual power to accomplish everyday victories.

I remember when my daughter Cassidy was in high school and faced many challenges to her faith from friends and teachers. As society redefined morality, Christians found themselves caught in the backlash against their viewpoints. She needed spiritual power to make it through school days—powerful peace, inspired words and responses, strategic ideas for getting along with others, and even ways of advancing the gospel there. I'm happy to say she overcame those challenges because she saw them as spiritual. God never intended believers to struggle through life with a lack of spiritual power. Because of the baptism in the Holy Spirit, we can thrive, not just scrape by. We can win even when things look weighted against us.

Destructive Demonic Influence

The New Testament speaks about spiritual power using two different words: *exousia* and *dunamis*. Exousia means authority, and dunamis means ability. Every believer has exousia from the moment we say yes to Jesus

Christ. This is what I like to call "positional power." We sit in a position with Jesus, and our trust and faith in Him give us authority. We step into a place of authority immediately as His followers. But many Christians don't step into the ability, the dunamis, that baptism in the Holy Spirit provides. I like to call this "transactional power." It is the power to make things happen according to the will and Word of God. No devil can stop the power of God, the power of the Holy Spirit. Christians who don't access this power remain weakened and confused in the face of battles God meant for them to gloriously win.

When Freedom House Church was just a few years old and had around fifty people attending on Sunday mornings, a family with two kids began to come to services. They were a little bit of a mess, and we prayed for them a lot. For some reason, the father had an extremely difficult time receiving the Holy Spirit. His wife, on the other hand, received the baptism readily, and it frustrated him that after weeks of prayer, he still wasn't receiving this baptism.

One day I sat down with him to inquire about his background, and he told me his relatives had engaged in witchcraft and occult practices. After just a few minutes, I could see there was a lot of junk in his family's past.

"Let's break the influence of the past engagement of witchcraft and occult practices in your life because maybe it's holding you back," I said to him, wishing I had been smart enough to recognize this issue and deal with it earlier.

We prayed, and I took authority over the demonic influences, spirits, and any residual power of witchcraft, false worship, and idolatry present in his life because of his lineage. Within seconds of our praying together, he received the baptism in the Holy Spirit and started praying in tongues. He couldn't stop. The floodgates opened, and he could hardly say one word in English for the next day or two! He prayed in tongues all night long and woke up praying in tongues. He couldn't even go to work the next day! It was like the Holy Spirit had been waiting for him to exercise authority as a believer to clean out spiritual obstacles, enabling him to flow in this wonderful gift.

But having lost a grip on this man, the devil went after his kids. In those days, we were a mobile church meeting in a school, so we had to set the church up and break it down each week. One Sunday, after packing up the church's equipment, Penny and I had gotten home late in the day when a minivan pulled up in front of my house.

I walked up to see how I could help them, and their son was writhing and thrashing around, manifesting demonic influence in the car! As they had tried to drive home, this kid had reached up and tried to choke his father to death. The scene was like something out of a bad horror movie, but having encountered this kind of demonic display before, I knew to confront it with power, both "positional" and "transactional."

"In Jesus' name, leave this boy," I commanded the demon.

Immediately, the boy calmed down, but I knew the demon was laying low and trying to hide so that I would leave it alone.

"Don't lie to me. You're not gone. You're just faking it," I said to the demon. The boy looked at me and said, "I'm not leaving."

Things were getting real!

"Yes, you are leaving, in the name of Jesus," I said.

He began ripping at the seats in the car. By now, my neighbors were coming over to see what was happening. The boy's parents didn't know what to do. I commanded again that the demon come out of the boy.

Immediately, he stopped being aggressive and calmed straight down. His face lit up as if he had just woken up. Honestly, it was amazing to see how oppressed this young man was and to see him completely change in front of us. It was nothing but the power of God.

We later found out that the teenage boy had been involved in pornography and very violent video games. This experience taught me that we must be careful not to open doors to evil spirits. They are very real and very destructive.

Dunamis Power and Authority

It shouldn't surprise you when you encounter this kind of situation. It happened to Jesus and the early Christians all the time. It happens today all around the world. Demons are alive and well on planet earth, even if they try to hide and do their work in darkness, so people don't suspect they're there.

I have news for you. You can't argue a demon out of someone's life. You can't preach one out or persuade it. It requires power—the dunamis power the New Testament talks about, received through the baptism in the Holy Spirit.

I know what you are thinking: "I am not going to run into some demon-possessed man at my bank job." And the truth is, you probably will not. But every day, we face pressure and opposition to God's plan for our lives as the enemy, the devil, is trying to stop you and hold you back. This is called spiritual warfare. It is very real, and we are engaged in it whether we like it or not. Either we are walking with the devil, or we are facing him head-on. When you become a Christian, you now have a bullseye on your back. You are a target for the powers of darkness and they want to take you out, hold you back, or oppress you in some way.

There is a great example of this in the ministry of Jesus. One day a Roman military leader who understood positional authority and transactional power came to Jesus (see Matthew 8). He pleaded with him to save the life of the centurion's valuable servant. Jesus offered to come to the centurion's house and heal the man, but the centurion answered profoundly, "Lord, I am not worthy that You should come under my roof. But only speak a word....For I also am a man under authority"—that is, exousia—"I say to this one, 'Go,' and he goes; and to another, 'Come,' and he comes; and to my servant, 'Do this,' and he does it."

Do you see the explanation of authority and power in his statement? He recognized the spiritual authority Jesus possessed. And he understood the power, which is the ability to exercise authority in a specific way, that Jesus had. Jesus healed the man's servant, but the mind-boggling thing is this: You and I stand in the same position of authority and power that Jesus did in that situation. Jesus sacrificed His life for us to bring us into partnership with Himself. The cross permits us to operate in the authority of Jesus by implementing His power over the kingdom of darkness. Jesus told a large group of disciples, "I give you the authority to trample on serpents and scorpions," by which He meant demonic powers (Luke 10:19). The disciples told Him, "Even the demons obey us!" (Luke 10:17, NLT).

We should be able to say the same thing. If we can't, then we are not operating in the power that our authority gives us. This power begins with receiving the baptism in the Holy Spirit.

Paul said that having disarmed principalities and powers by the cross, Jesus took away all their weaponry (Col. 2:14–15). Jesus had the authority to do this because He lived a perfect life and regained the title deed to the earth for Himself and His followers, which had been lost when Adam and Eve sinned. The cross of Christ puts us back in our original position of authority. When we speak the Word of God, things change in the spiritual realms of our marriages, families, job situations, neighborhoods, and more. Christians possess much more power than we typically exercise.

Remember that Jesus expressly said the baptism in the Holy Spirit would endue (cover and fill) His disciples with supernatural power (Luke 24:49). We must experience this same baptism to walk in that same power. When we do, we live life *under the influence*. When fighting with the enemy, we never have to think, "I hope I can defeat him." The reality is his authority has been stripped and won back by Jesus. The enemy is defeated, and our task is to remind him of his defeat and force him to relinquish power over people and circumstances.

We never fight *for* victory; we fight *from* victory.

Peter wrote, "Grace and peace be multiplied to you in the knowledge of God and of Jesus our Lord, as His divine power has given to us all things that pertain to life and godliness" (2 Pet. 1:2–3). The Greek word for power in this verse is—you guessed it—dunamis, that miracle-working power. It enables us to act in partnership with the Holy Spirit to order our lives and bring about kingdom results in every situation we are called to. Peter said, "All things that pertain to life and godliness" come under our authority. That's a broad scope for us to work in! Anything in your life and area of authority must submit to the power at work in you by the Holy Spirit, given through this third baptism. God will never send you into a situation without your having the power to implement His will.

Bringing Things to Light

When we exercise spiritual power, we partner with the Holy Spirit to convict the world of sin, draw people to Christ, and expose the enemy's presence and plans. Jesus said:

> And when He has come, He will convict the world of sin, and of righteousness, and of judgment; of sin, because they do not believe in Me; of righteousness, because I go to My Father and you see Me no more; of judgment, because the ruler of this world is judged.
>
> —John 16:8–11

The power of Christ brings everything to light—the motives of men and women, the work of the enemy and the righteousness of God. When things are exposed, we can properly assess them. The Bible calls this judging or judgment. This happened when the father in my earlier example prayed, and we evicted witchcraft and the occult from his life. We pronounced "judgment" on that influence. It continued when the enemy tried to claim his son but was exposed and sent away by commands given in spiritual authority. We pronounced "judgment" on the spirit that was influencing him.

Notice that the work of the Holy Spirit is to convict, which is to convince someone of the truth. I did not condemn that father or his son, nor does the Holy Spirit condemn us. He's not out to destroy or harm us but to rescue us by bringing darkness to the surface and banishing it from our lives. If you ever feel condemned and hopeless, remember this is always the enemy of your soul and not your friend, the Holy Spirit. Conviction will always lead us to God and to hope, not away from God into hopelessness. Condemnation isolates a person. Conviction always draws people closer to the light of God and fellowship with Him and other believers. Condemnation makes you feel guilty and full of shame. Conviction brings about the peace and love of God.

When we apply spiritual power and bring things into the light, we can see what is righteous and what is not. The Holy Spirit might convict people of living together before marriage, taking illegal or unhelpful substances, cheating at work, or whatever else originates in darkness. But he also exposes that which is praiseworthy and good. This gives us the confidence to continue living rightly and to exercise the power given through our authority in Christ. When you know that you're behaving righteously and that God celebrates this, you want to do it more boldly!

You Can Have Spiritual Discernment

How do we identify the enemy's work? The Bible tells us there is a spiritual gift called discernment. It is a lost gift in our day because of the prevalence of information available with a few internet searches. We think we know everything—or at least have access to all the answers—but this doesn't work in the spiritual realm. Only the Holy Spirit can give us the ability to discern which spirits are at work in a situation or a person. We need to ask God, not Google.

Discernment is a spiritual gift that operates in faith and provides superior and more-accurate information than we can apprehend through the five senses. It is information disclosed spiritually by the Holy Spirit. Sometimes discernment feels like a gentle suggestion or leading. At other times it is a strong response to an immediate spiritual problem, such as with the demonized boy.

Our job as followers of Jesus and partners of the Holy Spirit is to grow in spiritual discernment, having our "senses trained to discern good and evil" (Heb. 5:14, NASB). Churches have plenty of leaders well-trained in growth strategies, fund-raising, preaching, and so on, but the world desperately needs men and women who operate in power and the gift of discernment. It gives us accuracy in our exercise of power, allowing us to see the spiritual realities behind physical situations. It helps us hit the bullseye rather than fire blindly. Paul wrote, "Now He who searches the hearts knows what the mind of the Spirit is, because He makes intercession for the saints according to the will of God" (Rom. 8:27).

One of the great reasons to seek the baptism in the Holy Spirit is so you can discern and act with power in all situations. With that said, none of us should go overboard in demon-hunting. Not every situation or encounter is about sniffing out the enemy and confronting him. We had one family in our church who was super-spiritual and really into exercising the gift of discernment. But they took it to an extreme. They were always saying, "That's a demon. That's a demon." Finally, I asked them, "Do you ever see angels or anything good? The Bible says to discern both good and evil, not just evil."

The goal of exposing the enemy is not to make him our focus. We must fix our eyes on Jesus (Heb. 12:2). Being hyper-aware of the devil wrongly empowers him in our lives, and we get wrapped up in fear. God does not call us to be demon hunters and Holy Spirit barometers wherever we go. Instead, follow the leading of the Spirit of God, function under His influence, and let Him do the exposing.

We must be confident to stand in our God-given authority and operate in spiritual power, including everyday matters. One way to maintain readiness and an open ear to the Holy Spirit is by speaking in tongues, which I discuss next.

At the core, I believe discernment is not so much about deciding between what is right or wrong. It is knowing the difference between what is right and almost right. Or another way to look at it, is what is good and what is God. It is pretty easy to know right from wrong. It gets more difficult when something is good but we are not sure it is God's best for us. The Holy Spirit can help lead you in making that decision. Maybe you have some decisions right now you need help making.

Father, I need the gift of discernment in my life. I have some decisions that I am facing and need your direction and leadership. I open my heart up to your Spirit. Show me the way. In Jesus' name, amen.

Reflections for Further Study

1. What comes to mind when you hear the words *spiritual power*?

2. Do you operate in the power of the Holy Spirit as part of your walk with Christ? If so, what does that look like?

3. Describe a situation in which you acted in the power of the Holy Spirit to achieve an outcome. How did you know what to do? What was the result?

4. Consider this account of a powerful spiritual encounter in Paul's ministry in Philippi:

> Now it happened, as we went to prayer, that a certain slave girl possessed with a spirit of divination met us, who brought her masters much profit by fortune-telling. This girl followed Paul and us, and cried out, saying, "These men are the servants of the Most High God, who proclaim to us the way of salvation." And this she did for many days.
>
> But Paul, greatly annoyed, turned and said to the spirit, "I command you in the

> name of Jesus Christ to come out of her."
> And he came out that very hour.
>
> —Acts 16:16–18

5. Have you ever been involved in a confrontation with evil spirits? What happened, and how did the situation resolve?

CHAPTER 8

WHAT IS SPEAKING IN TONGUES?

ONE OF THE most misunderstood aspects of the baptism with the Holy Spirit is speaking in tongues. It remains a subject of needless contention and dispute, even as Pentecostal and Charismatic movements, which practice gifts of the Spirit, such as speaking in tongues, have grown to around seven hundred million people worldwide and continue to grow. Some Christians don't consider it necessary; others feel uneasy or afraid of this gift. Still, others have had bad experiences with people or situations where speaking in tongues was practiced or sought.

Most harmfully, some evangelical Christians even

claim that speaking in tongues is not meant for today. This amazes me not only because speaking in tongues is clearly biblical but because these people will talk all day long in earthly languages and think nothing of it. We must remember that at the time I'm writing this book, there are over seventy-one hundred earthly languages worldwide. If we believe God created this world, why would we hesitate to believe He would also create a heavenly language?

If you introduce the topic of heavenly languages or a spiritual prayer language to these leaders, they say it's not for believers. They keep people from understanding and receiving this important, empowering gift.

The truth is the roots of speaking in tongues go back to the very beginning of humanity, and the Word of God makes this clear. It's just that people don't have the desire or diligence to study it out and seek biblical understanding. They'd rather say, "God works in mysterious ways," and dismiss the topic with a shrug of the shoulders. I have news for them: God does not work in mysterious ways! He works according to His Word, and he explains His ways to us in His Word.

He does not ask Christians to blindly grope along, hoping we stumble upon the right teachings. Rather, He told us to study the Word of God and allow it to set our course and serve as our ultimate paradigm. We discover who God is and how He behaves every time we read the Bible. If anyone thinks God's ways are mysterious, that person hasn't read His Word enough to understand His ways.

I say this because speaking in tongues, like all biblical teachings, has a strong foundation in the Word of God—including in the Old Testament. In fact, every Christian doctrine or theological principle has a witness or precedent in the Old Testament. Whenever you study something in the New Testament, you can always find a type or shadow of it in the Old Testament. The Bible itself says truth is established in the mouths of two or three witnesses (Matt. 18:16). Jesus said he fulfilled the Law and the prophets (Matt. 5:17). This tells us biblical principles never stand alone from the rest of the witness of Scripture. The Bible is unified from Genesis to Revelation and speaks in unity about the gift of tongues.

Let's examine the scriptural foundation for speaking in tongues as an important aspect of the baptism with the Holy Spirit. You may be surprised by what the Word says about it.

The Tower of Babel

The roots or foundation of the doctrine of speaking in tongues go back to the Tower of Babel. The story is found in Genesis chapter 11 and opens with these words, "Now the whole earth had one language and one speech. And it came to pass, as they journeyed from the east, that they found a plain in the land of Shinar, and they dwelt there" (Gen. 11:1–2).

The name Shinar means "two rivers." So these opening verses tell us that the people then had one language and were traveling to a place of two rivers. We'll look at those facts more in a minute.

The biblical account goes on to say:

> Then they said to one another, "Come, let us make bricks and bake them thoroughly." They had brick for stone, and they had asphalt for mortar. And they said, "Come, let us build ourselves a city, and a tower whose top is in the heavens; let us make a name for ourselves, lest we be scattered abroad over the face of the whole earth."
>
> —GENESIS 11:3–4

Acting in pride, all nations of the world decided to build a tower that reached the heavens, to make a name for themselves. They didn't want to partner with God; they wanted to take the place of God. They wanted to be fully independent of their Maker, and they were going to prove it by building a grand, towering structure to magnify their name.

The next five verses tell us God's reaction.

> But the LORD came down to see the city and the tower which the sons of men had built. And the LORD said, "Indeed the people are one and they all have one language, and this is what they begin to do; now nothing that they propose to do will be withheld from them. Come, let Us go down and there confuse their language, that they may not understand one another's speech." So the LORD scattered them abroad from there over the face

> of all the earth, and they ceased building the city. Therefore its name is called Babel, because there the LORD confused the language of all the earth; and from there the LORD scattered them abroad over the face of all the earth.
>
> –GENESIS 11:5–9

Humanity was powerful when it shared one common language. When God fragmented and "confused" human speech into many languages, it stripped the nations of the power to come together to carry out great and prideful plans. Many Christians take this as an interesting, stand-alone story from ancient history, but in fact, it is foundational to the purpose of God for humanity and to the purpose of speaking in tongues today.

REVERSING THE CURSE OF BABEL

In Genesis 11 people pursued the wrong plan and purpose and united in corruption and pride. The Father, Son, and Holy Spirit united to confuse the languages at Babel and keep the human race from accomplishing great but misguided goals. But God never intended to leave humanity in a weakened, ineffective state. Rather, God created mankind to powerfully carry out every good purpose for the earth in unity and strength.

Remember, God's original command to humanity was to have dominion. God did not abandon that plan but postponed it by creating confusion at Babel. Two thousand years later He hit the "play" button again to begin to re-unify the languages of mankind and reconnect us to our original purpose under the leadership of Jesus and the Holy Spirit. Here's how it happened: "When the Day of Pentecost had fully come, they were all with one accord in one place" (Acts 2:1).

It's important to see that the disciples' motivation was right. They were in righteous unity with God and with one another. Their purpose was to fulfill the great commission, and they were waiting patiently for the empowerment to do that. They had heard from Jesus and were obedient to His direction.

The next verse says, "And suddenly there came a sound from heaven, as of a rushing mighty wind, and it filled the whole house where they were sitting" (v. 2). God had breathed life into Adam to create the first living person. Now He breathed life into this group to create the first church on earth, the body of Christ. With the breath of God in their lungs, they now had the capacity to speak a spiritual language, which brought unprecedented power and unity to their group and their message.

It goes on to say, "Then there appeared to them divided tongues as of fire" (v. 3). Remember Shinar from the Tower of Babel? It means "two rivers." Now we encounter the Greek word *diamerizo*, which means "distributed, cloven, twofold." It is the same concept. Shinar was a prophetic indicator that the baptism with the Holy Spirit would involve a twofold purpose for speaking heavenly languages. One purpose is a personal language or personal prayer language, and one is a public language for blessing the church, the gift of tongues with interpretation. We will examine these more in a moment.

The next verse tells us, "And they were all filled with the Holy Spirit and began to speak with other tongues, as the Spirit gave them utterance" (v. 4). It's important to note something I'll discuss later in more detail—and that is, they began to speak. The Holy Spirit didn't take over their mouths and force them to talk. This was not some kind of heavenly possession.

Everything we do with the Holy Spirit is a partnership. If you are unwilling, it won't happen. So they had to do their part and speak as the Spirit gave them utterance. The Holy Spirit is always a gentleman; He only operates where He is invited. *We never lose our will with Him. We simply yield our will to Him.*

> And there were dwelling in Jerusalem Jews, devout men, from every nation under heaven. And when this sound occurred, the multitude came together, and were confused, because everyone heard them speak in his own language. Then they were all amazed and marveled, saying to one another, "Look, are not all these who speak Galileans? And how is it that we hear, each in our own language in which we were born? Parthians and Medes and Elamites, those dwelling in Mesopotamia, Judea and Cappadocia, Pontus and Asia, Phrygia and Pamphylia, Egypt and the parts of Libya adjoining Cyrene, visitors from Rome, both Jews and proselytes, Cretans and Arabs—we hear them speaking in our own tongues the wonderful

> works of God." So they were all amazed and perplexed, saying to one another, "Whatever could this mean?"
>
> Others mocking said, "They are full of new wine."
>
> But Peter, standing up with the eleven, raised his voice and said to them, "Men of Judea and all who dwell in Jerusalem, let this be known to you, and heed my words. For these are not drunk, as you suppose, since it is only the third hour of the day. But this is what was spoken by the prophet Joel:
>
> —ACTS 2:5–16

What was the Holy Spirit doing here by speaking to men of many nationalities through people who had never learned those languages? He was beginning to reverse the curse of Genesis 11 by giving humanity a language to communicate with God and one another more profoundly than ever before. He was pointing us back to God's original purpose for humanity to speak and act as one body in total unity under his leadership. He demonstrated this in the first group of Christians, who were in one accord with each other, in patient submission to God under the influence of the Holy Spirit.

While the men in Jerusalem that day did not recognize what was happening, it had been foretold seven hundred years earlier by their prophet, Zephaniah. He wrote: "For then I will restore to the peoples a pure language, that they all may call on the name of the LORD, to serve Him with one accord" (Zeph. 3:9).

United language—or, as *The Message* Bible puts it, "a language undistorted, unpolluted"—has always been part of God's plan for humans to communicate and work with Him to fulfill His great purposes. These purposes continue in our time and will ultimately be fulfilled when Jesus returns. Speaking in tongues is part of God's reunification and reempowerment process as He redeems humanity to accomplish what He created us to do from the beginning.

Two Types of Tongues

We've established a solid basis for the theological, practical, and prophetic importance of speaking in tongues, so let's dive into using this gift in our lives and churches. Let's look in some depth at chapters 12–14 of 1 Corinthians, which I have heard described this way:

> Chapter 12 is about the gifts of the Spirit.
>
> Chapter 13 is about the spirit of the gifts (love).
>
> Chapter 14 is about the language of the Spirit.

These are great chapters to study as you seek and receive the baptism with the Holy Spirit and this awesome gift of tongues, our prayer language. In these chapters, Paul tells us there are two types of speaking in tongues: personal edification (betterment) and public proclamation (decree).

Apparently, the church in Corinth was brimming

with enthusiasm for exercising the gifts of the Spirit, including the gifts of tongues and interpretation. But they were so new to it that they created an environment of disorder and confusion. Like any good pastor, Paul instructed them when and how these gifts were to be used so that all were built up in the Spirit. Keep in mind that most of Paul's letters were written to entire churches and were likely read aloud to all believers in a particular city. So this letter served as a public teaching and correction of what was happening in this very young, excited church.

Let me summarize his teaching on speaking in tongues. Paul said there are two aspects of this gift: speaking in tongues in a person's personal prayer life and speaking in tongues with the interpretation in a church setting for the benefit of everyone. Confusion can arise when we don't identify which type of tongues Paul refers to throughout chapters 12, 13, and 14. People's ignorance and neglect of this fact have led to incalculable misunderstandings about how the gift of tongues functions in church settings and our lives. We must understand the difference between the two exercises of the gift of tongues so we can operate in the power of each.

Paul began:

> Now concerning spiritual gifts, brethren, I do not want you to be ignorant...There are diversities of gifts, but the same Spirit. There are differences of ministries, but the same Lord. And there

> are diversities of activities, but it is the same God who works all in all.
>
> —1 Corinthians 12:1, 4–6

Paul's first point was that because all gifts and activities flow from the Holy Spirit, they will never conflict with one another and cause disorder or confusion. Other parts of the New Testament tell us the Holy Spirit has given believers nine gifts, which I like to group into three categories:

1. power gifts: faith, healing, and miracles
2. revelation gifts: word of wisdom, word of knowledge, and discerning of the spirits
3. speaking gifts: prophecy, tongues, and interpretation of tongues

Each of these gifts is valuable and powerful, and believers can rest assured that they all have one giver—the Holy Spirit—who beautifully orchestrates their use within a church through the life of a believer.

Paul then says there are "different kinds of tongues" (v. 10). A few verses later, he refers to "varieties of tongues" (v. 28) and then to "the tongues of men and of angels" (13:1). Clearly, speaking in tongues is a gift with multiple aspects under one heading. The divided tongues of fire that appeared over the disciples' heads in Acts 2 symbolized this.

Paul then explained how the gift of tongues functions in the life of a church. In a public arena, he said, prophecy was preferable to the personal exercise of tongues but not to the public practice of giving a message in tongues with an accompanying interpretation.

If anyone stood up in a church meeting and spoke in tongues without an interpretation, it would make no sense to the hearers and would do them no good. Worse, if newcomers came to that church meeting, they would conclude that Christians were crazy. Apparently, this was happening in Corinth as enthusiastic believers spoke in tongues in corporate settings without any interpretations.

Some Christians today do not distinguish between the personal and the corporate (group) function of tongues, so they associate speaking in tongues with public disorder and reject it entirely. This is unbiblical and not the will of God for any church. It springs from bias and unnecessary confusion about this gift.

In the early days of planting Freedom House Church, I helped lead worship with a piecemeal band while searching for the right person to take over that ministry. The band practiced and prayed together on Saturday nights and before services on Sunday mornings. One day we circled up to pray on Sunday morning. When I pray alone or with small groups of people, I call out to God in English and allow my personal prayer language to flow as well, praying in tongues. I "pray with the spirit, and I will also pray with the understanding," as Paul wrote (1 Cor. 14:15).

One Sunday, one of the band members approached me after our prayer time. "It makes me uncomfortable when you pray in tongues," he said. "I'd rather you not do it." This surprised me, even though I knew some people in our church hadn't experienced this gift before.

"I didn't know it made you so uncomfortable," I told him.

"Well, my understanding is that if you pray in tongues, there should always be an interpretation," he said.

"That's true in a public setting, but I'm praying in my private prayer language," I said.

"It still makes me uncomfortable," he said. "If you keep doing it, my family won't be able to attend this church."

Losing his family meant losing six people, more than ten percent of our church at the time.

"I'm sorry," I said. "I'd hate to lose you, but I'm not going to stop."

The man and his family never came back—all because he had a wrong understanding of the twofold exercise of the gift of tongues. In a corporate setting, he was correct. There must always be an interpretation of tongues spoken to a group. The Bible is clear about that. But his perspective denied using tongues as a personal prayer language except when someone was completely alone.

Your Personal Prayer Language

In the next chapter, we will look in more depth at the personal practice of speaking in tongues. To conclude here, let me make a couple of important general points.

First, Paul encouraged both exercises of the gift of tongues, writing, "I wish you all spoke with tongues" (1

Cor. 14:5). He asserted, "I speak with tongues more than you all," and commanded, "do not forbid to speak with tongues" (vv. 18, 39) because he knew how powerful a personal prayer language is.

Let me assure you that this gift of tongues is meant for every believer. While not all will give public messages in tongues, I believe all can and should seek a personal prayer language that God offers to us as part of the baptism with the Holy Spirit. The Bible calls it speaking in tongues, praying in tongues, praying in the spirit, singing in the spirit, and many other descriptions. All refer to the same gift—this personal language God gives us.

Second, I do not believe that speaking in tongues is the only evidence of being baptized in the Holy Spirit and living under His influence. The church where I met the Lord and first grew in my faith taught that when you were baptized in the Holy Spirit, you spoke in tongues; if you did not speak in tongues, then you hadn't received this baptism. I consider that to be a misconception. I believe any spiritual gift is evidence of the baptism in the Holy Spirit. No single one is the only evidence of the baptism with the Holy Spirit. I know many people who don't speak in tongues who are far more Spirit-filled than those who do!

I heard a man say long ago, "You never pick out shoes because of the tongues." In the same way, each of us should seek baptism in the Holy Spirit without making tongues the central issue. That said, speaking in tongues has many wonderful benefits that we will cover in the following chapter.

Gifts Don't Equal Character

I noticed as I grew in the Lord that some people who speak in tongues don't live godly lives in other areas. In other words, the gifts of the Spirit are not a measure of the fruit of the Spirit (Gal. 5:22–23). I have observed that they're not necessarily even related. For example, I know people who do not pray in tongues but have all kinds of love, joy, peace, patience, kindness, goodness, faithfulness, gentleness, and self-control working in their lives. I've known others who spoke in tongues and operated in other gifts of the Spirit and seemed to have none of the fruit of the Spirit. They didn't have much love for other people and probably didn't even like themselves!

Whom would you rather spend time with—someone who can speak in tongues and prophesy all day long but has no love or peace, or someone whose character reflects the character of God, described in the fruit of the Spirit? I know whom I would choose.

We do well to remember that Jesus said the key evidence of the baptism with the Holy Spirit is that we are witnesses of Him. This means our character also reflects His character. Some people become enamored of their gifts and make those the focus of attention. But all gifts, including tongues in any setting, must put attention on Jesus, not ourselves or others. That is being a witness. Our character testifies to the influence and power of the

Holy Spirit in us. We should not and must not elevate supernatural gifts over these other evidences.

Most important of all is love. All gifts must operate primarily in love. Love is the motivation for speaking in tongues in personal and corporate settings. It is the ultimate witness of God being active in your life.

Now that it's clear from the Word of God that the gift of tongues operates in two distinct ways, personal edification (betterment) and public proclamation (decree), let's take a look at the many benefits this gift brings to us in our personal lives.

> *Father in heaven, I want to understand more about the Holy Spirit and His gifts. Please open my eyes and my understanding as I continue to study the Scriptures. Open Your Word to me in Jesus' name, amen.*

Reflections for Further Study

1. How were you introduced to the doctrine and practice of speaking in tongues? What were your initial thoughts about it?

2. Speaking in tongues is sometimes characterized as divisive by modern Christian teachers. But in what ways does the Bible indicate that this spiritual gift is powerfully unifying?

3. What are the two types of tongues? Explain as if to someone who does not know.

4. Consider this description of the early church after the apostles were threatened by religious leaders:

> They raised their voice to God with one accord....And when they had prayed, the place where they were assembled together was shaken; and they were all filled with the Holy Spirit, and they spoke the word of God with boldness.
>
> Now the multitude of those who believed were of one heart and one soul; neither did anyone say that any of the things he possessed was his own, but they had all things in common. And with

> great power the apostles gave witness to the resurrection of the Lord Jesus. And great grace was upon them all.
>
> —Acts 4:24, 31–33

5. Based on this passage, what are some characteristics of a church "filled with the Holy Spirit"? How do they behave? In what ways are they described here?

CHAPTER 9

RECEIVING THE GIFT OF TONGUES

Like anyone new to the practice of this gift, people want to know why they should desire the gift of tongues, how it benefits them, and how to do it. Let's look at specific reasons the Bible gives every believer for seeking and receiving this empowering experience.

You Can Pray God's Perfect Will

The first benefit—and it's huge—is that praying in tongues allows us to pray God's perfect will for our lives. Paul writes, "For he who speaks in a tongue does not speak to men but to God, for no one understands him; however, in the spirit he speaks mysteries" (1 Cor. 14:2).

The word *mystery* does not mean something God intends to keep secret from us. Rather, it means something we don't know until we ask God for understanding. A mystery is something God wants to reveal about our lives, Himself, or the world around us. Think of mysteries as divine information God wants to share with you when you are ready to handle it.

So what does it mean to speak mysteries? Put simply, it means that when you pray in tongues, you pray God's perfect will over your life. We all want to know and pray for God's best for us. We all want to understand the direction we should take. We all want to discover God's purposes for us. When we pray in tongues, we ask Him for these things. We put our deepest requests before God and pull those mysteries—those answers—into our present reality by faith. We connect the heart of God to the concrete circumstances of our lives. This is how intercession works, and praying in tongues is the mechanism by which we agree with and ask for God's perfect will.

How do we know what to pray? We don't, but the Holy Spirit does, and He does it through our mouths when we speak in tongues. Paul says: "Now He who searches the hearts knows what the mind of the Spirit is, because He [the Holy Spirit] makes intercession for the saints according to the will of God" (Rom. 8:27).

Speaking in tongues is like a hotline from our spirit to God. We don't have to know what to pray for because the Spirit makes intercession through us in "groanings which cannot be uttered" (v. 26). He supplies the prayers, and the Father supplies the answers. When I don't know how to pray for my finances, relationships, or health, the Holy Spirit knows. My feelings say one thing, and my mind says another—but what I really need is the mind of God for each area of my life. When you pray in tongues, you speak the perfect will of God into the physical realm. You intercede precisely for your life and other matters.

Praying in tongues bypasses our limited minds. For those of us whose logic sometimes gets in the way, speaking in tongues is the ultimate workaround! Paul says we don't understand what we are praying for. To say it another way, our fallen, corrupted reason no longer defines the conversation with God or gets in the way of effectively communicating with Him. Whatever might rise up in my brain to question or doubt the plans of God gets brushed aside. Under the perfect influence of the Holy Spirit, my spirit prays God's awesome will without interference or second-guessing.

I am not demeaning the minds God gave us, but we have to face the reality that while our spirits have been made perfect because of the sacrifice Jesus made for us, our understanding is still being saved, being redeemed. The Bible calls it sanctification and also the renewing of our minds. This means our minds are a work in progress. For this reason, we should want our spirits to be more engaged in prayer than our minds.

This is why Paul wrote, "For if I pray in a tongue, my

spirit prays, but my understanding is unfruitful" (1 Cor. 14:14). Some people read that and say, "What's the use of praying if I don't understand what I'm saying?" In essence, Paul says, "While your sinful mind is going through the process of being renewed, God gives us a way to pray perfectly with our redeemed spirits." This is a big deal. If you have ever wanted to pray perfectly, rejoice that God gave us the means to do so through the gift of tongues.

I find this to be ultimately practical. When I have a business or ministry situation I don't know how to handle, I pray in tongues. If there's a personal challenge, I pray in tongues. I set it before God and speak mysteries to Him in the inspired language of the Spirit.

My perspective on my own life is so limited. His is unlimited and omniscient. I see very little. He sees everything, and He knows my future. When I pray in tongues, I ask Him to perfectly address my life situations in the best way possible—which only He can know.

Praying in tongues also gives me peace that I have done the best I can. I offer it to Him, and the solution is not up to me anymore, though undoubtedly, He will tell me to do certain things as He guides me. When I pray in tongues, I bring God into the situation and allow Him to take the lead. I put myself totally under His influence.

Can we pray with our understanding as well? Yes. Paul says, "I will pray with the spirit, and I will also pray with the understanding" (v. 15). It isn't one or the other. But Paul valued the gift of tongues so highly that he told the Corinthian church, "I speak with tongues more than you all" (v. 18). He said he also sang in tongues, which is a great way to exercise this gift (1 Cor. 14:15). Speaking in tongues was a powerful aspect of this mighty apostle's life and ministry and should be for ours as well.

When You Need Strength

Speaking in tongues also edifies us, as Paul wrote. This means that praying or singing in the spirit builds us up and fortifies our minds, souls, and even bodies. Every morning I wake up knowing I need divine strength to be a better father, husband, leader, and follower of Jesus. Speaking in tongues equips me with greater strength. When I pray in tongues, the Holy Spirit gives me the power and insight to live, make decisions, and deal with daily circumstances and challenges.

I like how the apostle Paul puts it: "A person who speaks in tongues is strengthened personally" (1 Cor. 14:4, NLT). The Bible also says it this way: "But you, beloved, building yourselves up on your most holy faith, praying in the Holy Spirit" (Jude 20).

Praying in tongues fortifies our choice to build our lives on the foundation of Jesus Christ. This is the faith Jude refers to, and amazingly, praying in tongues builds us up in this faith. It is like strengthening a structure so it is stable and functions at its peak potential. To pray in tongues is to improve and enhance our lives of faith, built on the foundation of Christ himself.

Because Paul does not strictly define how speaking in tongues edifies us, we can assume he means it broadly. I believe speaking in tongues brings wholeness and health to every aspect of our lives, even our physical lives. God has a plan for our bodies, minds, and souls. He will lead us and give us wisdom in every area.

Connecting You to the Supernatural

Praying in tongues also keeps us in tune with spiritual realities. When I pray in tongues, I desensitize myself from the world's noise and sensitize myself to the leadings of God. I disconnect myself from things that typically pull me into the world's way of thinking and am drawn into how God thinks.

I believe Paul prayed in the spirit so much to keep himself in tune with the Holy Spirit and His purposes in every situation. Speaking in tongues puts you in a conversation with God so that when you step into a room, onto a platform, or into any situation, you are ready to operate in the Spirit immediately. Your words and actions are more likely to be an extension of your interaction with God, so you are ready to speak and serve and do what is good and needed.

I find that speaking in tongues throughout the day helps me experience and exercise the other gifts of the Spirit as well. It opens the door for the supernatural to operate more readily. Otherwise, we default to our natural minds for solutions. You never know when you might need a miracle, a healing, a prophetic word. You never know when you might need a word of wisdom or extra faith in a challenging situation. When I pray in the Spirit, those options seem closer at hand because I am already under His influence. This spiritual gift helps me turn down the world's noise and turn up the volume of God.

Common Questions

Let's briefly look at some questions people have about this gift.

1. When we talk about speaking in tongues, do we mean earthly or heavenly languages?

The answer is both! In Acts 2 the disciples spoke in human languages they had never learned but that were inspired by the Holy Spirit. Paul called these "tongues of men" (1 Cor. 13:1). They served as a sign and a wonder to the foreigners listening.

But Paul also referred to tongues of angels. Amazingly, our prayer languages include languages of heaven. This is a vast subject about which we know little, but given God's infinite diversity and creativity, we can safely speculate that there is not just one language in heaven but many. It also seems clear in Paul's statement that we do speak in tongues of angels when we speak in tongues, personally and corporately. That's pretty exciting!

A few years back we were in a prayer meeting at our new campus. We were all praying—some in tongues, some in English, and some in Spanish. I was praying in tongues. After the prayer meeting, a young lady approached me and said she heard me in the middle of my praying in tongues, saying things in Spanish as well. I don't know Spanish! Well, maybe a few things, but not what I was saying. Matter of fact, she said I was saying full sentences about the power of God in Spanish. Amazing!

2. Is it OK to pray in the spirit during worship or in other semi-public situations, such as small-group meetings?

Absolutely. God did not intend to limit our personal prayer languages to the closet. When we speak in tongues around others, it's usually part of our personal prayers to God, and we are not broadcasting them in a way that directs or interrupts what's happening corporately. It's fine if people overhear you, and they don't need an interpretation. When I pray on the microphone at the end of a church service, I sometimes let English and my prayer language flow freely and intermingle. I am not expecting the gift of tongues in that setting to serve a public function. The prayers are personal, even if others overhear them.

It is also appropriate in certain circumstances for someone to share a message in tongues in a corporate setting, as long as there is an interpretation. This requires the leadership of a pastor who is sensitive to the Holy Spirit at that moment, and it can be very edifying for a body of believers.

3. Did Jesus speak in tongues? After all, He was baptized in the Holy Spirit.

My best answer to that is no. Jesus didn't need a supernatural language to commune with the Father because He was in perfect communion already. He never fell out of a relationship with God. Jesus did not need supernatural language to bypass a corrupted mind. He did not need the curse of Genesis 11 reversed in His life. The Bible never indicates that Jesus spoke in tongues; in fact, Paul says speaking in tongues will one day cease (1 Cor. 13:8). This means they are part of our current experience in a fallen state but will not be after we are perfected. In my view, because Jesus has always been perfect, He did not need to speak in tongues to communicate perfectly with the Father.

The Experience of a Skeptic

A young man named William, who started on our worship team and became our church's youth leader, had many questions about the experience of speaking in tongues. He was from a Baptist background—we love Baptists!—and had grown up hearing things like, "Baptists can build a great chimney but can't start a fire. Pentecostals can start a fire but can't build a chimney, and they burn the whole house down." The Holy Spirit, in William's view, wasn't active in the lives of believers today except to introduce them to Jesus and to convict them of sin. This is a common mindset among evangelical Christians.

At Freedom House, we function vibrantly in the gifts of the Spirit and have open conversations about people's doubts and questions. William liked what he was hearing about living a life empowered by God and doing amazing things through the Holy Spirit—but he was, shall we say, quite reluctant about the baptism with the Holy Spirit and especially the gift of tongues. In his words, the gift of tongues was "for wackos."

One evening, a bunch of people came to my house for a Bible study and started hammering me with their toughest questions about tongues and the baptism with the Holy Spirit. William was one of them, and I could sense a yearning in his heart for something his head couldn't explain yet. William didn't just have a lot of reservations—he had a lot of fear and didn't know why. Tongues scared him, but his heart kept being pulled toward the subject.

"I knew there was something else," he told me later. "I knew I was hovering at a lower level and could go much farther."

His family discouraged him from seeking the baptism with the Holy Spirit, but without many concrete reasons. They just said things like, "I don't know about all that stuff." They stoked his fear. But after asking all his questions, William realized it was time to decide how to move forward. He knew he could read a thousand books and have a thousand conversations, but nothing more would happen until he took a step toward this gift.

At one of our men's events, he decided to act in child-like faith and see what happened. He came up to me and asked for prayer to receive the baptism with the Holy Spirit. In truth, he was freaked out. He didn't know what to expect, but he told himself, "Either I can choose to try to reason everything out and make it all make sense, or I can just go for it." He went for it, and a great peace came upon him as I prayed for him.

William received the baptism with the Holy Spirit and the gift of tongues, and he says today that he sees massive changes in his life, relationships, and everything about himself as a direct result. "I can see a significant difference when I'm operating with the Holy Spirit as opposed to years ago when it was just me," he said.

He advanced quickly in numerous areas, including ministry, which is why we hired him to lead our youth.

Things That Block the Holy Spirit's Work

What blocks us from receiving the baptism with the Holy Spirit? Sometimes it's tradition or fear, as William experienced. Another big one is unforgiveness and unresolved bitterness. Pride is a major hindrance, as are things like a history of occult practices, as we saw earlier, or generational curses passed down in our families.

The good news is all of these are easy to overcome with repentance. The main reason things remain blocked is that we get used to them and forget they're there. We don't realize we're still bitter or holding onto something unhelpful. We live in a state of offense. The Holy Spirit will bring these blockages to our attention so we can renounce them and move past them. Often it helps to say out loud: "I forgive my dad. I forgive my husband. I forgive my wife. I forgive my friend." Or, "I renounce all witchcraft and black magic my family has engaged in."

At our church, we make room for people to experience the gifts of the Spirit. We regularly invite people to receive prayer to be baptized in the Holy Spirit. I want an empowered church made up of Jesus followers living at peak performance by walking under the perfect influence of the Holy Spirit. We do not shy away from the activity of the Holy Spirit. While most Sunday services are about teaching and bringing in a harvest of new believers, we have a service called Encounter specifically to worship God and exercise the gifts of the Spirit in a larger setting. We pray for the sick to be healed and for people to experience the freedom that God has for us. We lay hands on people to receive the baptism in the Holy Spirit. We explain what's going on so people learn as it happens. We de-mystify it and make the supernatural normal.

When we welcome the Holy Spirit into the life of a church, He freely moves wherever and whenever people meet. The gifts of prophecy and words of wisdom occur in conversations in places like the grocery store, park, or at someone's house. Some people don't even realize the gifts are functioning; they just know they get blessed and encouraged by someone from our church.

You Can Receive Now

It's a good time to set the question before you: Do you want to receive this baptism, and would you like to receive it now? It can happen anywhere. You don't need to respond to an altar call or be at a church service. You can be alone or with others. What's required of you is simply faith. Nothing else. Not even a ton of faith. In fact, the same faith that got you saved will get you baptized in the Holy Spirit. It doesn't require an extra measure of faith or a new kind of faith. You simply walk in the faith you've already expressed toward God and invite Him to baptize you.

Perhaps you are sensing His presence and urging right now. I want to encourage you to pray this prayer or something like it:

> *Lord Jesus, thank You that You sent Your Holy Spirit to baptize me into the body of Christ. Now with that same faith, I ask to receive the baptism with the Holy Spirit. Lord Jesus, You are the Baptizer, so baptize me now with Your Holy Spirit.*

Linger in that prayer as long as you need to. Stay in an environment of faith and exercise tenacity right now. He likes it when we desire the things He wants to give us, so keep praying. Maybe repeat the prayer above and let God move on you.

I always find it useful to thank God for what He's done, so I also pray,

> *Thank You, God, for loving me and giving me good gifts. I want to receive all You have for me. Thank You for the Holy Spirit and the amazing ways He works in and through our lives. Fill me now with Your Holy Spirit.*

You may feel the desire to speak rising inside of you. Go ahead and speak without fear. Let His praise and His words come up from your spirit. What comes forth may be a new language. There is no right or wrong way to receive. Just continue to speak and thank and praise Him. He will give you the words in a language known or unknown.

When I was baptized in the Holy Spirit, I didn't feel overwhelming emotions, but I did start speaking in tongues. It was interesting and very liberating. Your experience may be different than mine. Just take time, open your mouth, and continue to pray. If the words sound unlike any you've ever heard or said before, let it happen. Stay in that time of prayer as long as you like. He will lead you through it. Remember, it is an act of your will; the Holy Spirit is a gentleman. He will not make you do anything you don't want or desire to do. Just start to pray for what is in your heart.

PRACTICE YOUR GIFT

Just as our relationship with the Father matures and develops over time, so it is with the Holy Spirit and our prayer language. The more you pray in tongues, the easier it flows. When you were born, you didn't come out saying, "Hey, Mom. What's up, Dad?" It took you took a while to develop language skills.

That's how it is with any foreign language—it takes time. I took five years of French in high school and college but can barely speak any now because I didn't keep it up. I didn't practice. The only way to become fluent in French is to go to France for a few months. You can sit in a classroom all your life, but you won't be proficient until you rely on a language for regular living.

It's the same with the language of the Spirit. Exercise it. Develop it. Work it like a muscle. Make it a normal habit. Become comfortable doing it. That's when you'll see dramatic life changes as a result. When you're in the car or taking a walk, pray in tongues and let it flow. In nearly all cases, you will have to start speaking. God won't do it for you. He is not a puppet master moving your mouth and vocal cords. He gave us a priceless gift of free will and will not make us do something we don't want to do.

Many people miss this point. Speaking in tongues is an act of your will. It's like a water spigot. The water is there and ready to come out, but it won't come out unless you turn the spigot. When you start to pray, you may feel something coming up in your belly. Jesus foretold this when He said, "Out of his heart will flow rivers of living water" (John 7:38). But you decide if that flowing river will come out of your mouth. You control the valve. The Holy Spirit will not move your jaw, lips, and tongue. You have to do it.

This means you can pray in tongues anytime you

want. You simply turn the spigot and let the river rise up and flow out of your mouth. You can stop whenever you want. (Now and then, in a very few special circumstances, the language flows so powerfully that it feels impossible to stop. This happened to the man who received the baptism after renouncing his family's occult history.)

The more I speak in tongues—turning the flow on, working that muscle, practicing the language that comes forth—the more open heaven seems to be, the more sensitive I am to the presence of God and the less sin I desire. I become more righteousness-conscious than sin-conscious. I am under the influence of the Holy Spirit Himself. Paul told the Thessalonians to "pray without ceasing" (1 Thess. 5:17). He meant to always position yourself to think, feel, and see as God does—to remain under His influence. I aim to keep myself in the right position of sensing, hearing, and enjoying God. The gift of tongues is a great help in that endeavor.

When I played baseball and softball, the coach moved me from infield to outfield, depending on the circumstances and players. Whenever I took the field, I had to know my position, the game situation, who was batting, and what kind of pitch our pitcher would throw. I stood in a certain place if a guy was on first base. If there was a runner on second or third, that affected where I stood. So did the number of outs, the inning, and if a left-handed slugger had just stepped to the plate.

Staying in position with God is a mindset that manifests in multiple habits, of which speaking in tongues is one. I consider it critical to functioning at a high level in the Christian life.

Being in position also means being around others who believe in the baptism with the Holy Spirit and speaking in tongues. If you are out of step with others about it, and they discourage you from keeping it up, it's more likely you won't turn that spigot and flow in the prayer language God gives you. You will come under their influence rather than the influence of the Holy Spirit. In fact, the enemy often tries to discourage people right after they receive the baptism.

Beware of the Deceiver

As soon as I got in the car after receiving the baptism of the Holy Spirit, it was like the devil sat beside me and said, "That wasn't real. That was fake. It was gibberish." Somehow I knew that anything the devil tells you is a lie, so the best strategy is to do exactly the opposite of what he says. He told me speaking in tongues wasn't real, so I began speaking in tongues more! I still do that thirty years later when the devil tries to tell me it's not real—and he tries on occasion.

When you wake up in the morning and feel that unction to pray, don't let the devil talk you out of it. Put yourself fully under the influence of the Holy Spirit. Turn on the faucet, and let the words flow from within you as Jesus promised. Pray and sing in the spirit and watch how God elevates your life, joy, and experience of

Him. He will take you higher and farther when you are in a position to receive from Him.

As soon as possible, find a good church that believes in the exercise of the gifts. If you are in a church that doesn't practice or believe in these things, don't beat up your pastor about it. Let him pursue God in the best way he knows how. It's not your job to change the minds of your church leadership. Rather, let the Lord lead you in this new way. God will lead you to the right church if you're walking in obedience. Find a mentor and join a small group if you can. These relationships will support what God is doing in your life.

I am excited about what God has in store for you as you live more and more under the influence of the Holy Spirit!

Reflections for Further Study

1. What are the three biblical benefits of speaking in tongues Paul lists in 1 Corinthians 14:2?

2. If you have never spoken in tongues before, are you open to doing so? Explain why and what you hope to gain.

3. What steps can you take right now to put yourself in circumstances that encourage the baptism with the Holy Spirit and speaking in tongues?

4. Consider these excerpts from 1 Corinthians 14:

   - I wish you all spoke with tongues, but even more that you prophesied (v. 5).

   - I will pray with the spirit, and I will also pray with the understanding. I will sing with the spirit, and I will also sing with the understanding. (v. 15).

   - I thank my God I speak with tongues more than you all (v. 18).

- Therefore, brethren, desire earnestly to prophesy, and do not forbid to speak with tongues. Let all things be done decently and in order. (vv. 39–40).

5. Have you ever "forbidden" yourself from speaking in tongues due to some incorrect doctrine, fear, or misunderstanding? Do you desire to pray and sing in the spirit the way Paul describes? Begin by thanking God for this gift, and then posture yourself to receive from Him all that He has to give you—including the baptism with the Holy Spirit and the gift of a personal prayer language.

CONCLUSION

The Bible says to continually be filled with the Holy Spirit—to be under His influence. This means we regularly experience fresh infillings like renewals of our original baptism. For this reason, always be in a posture of seeking and receiving. I fervently believe that the first thing you should do when you wake up is pray, worship God, and read your Bible. Even if you are not a morning person, these things should precede your other activities.

I compare it to tuning your instrument before you play it. Many people go into their day out of tune, so everything they do sounds off. Musicians know that you can play the right chords or hit the right strings, but if the instrument is out of tune, it will sound bad no matter how accurate you are. That's why I ask Jesus to baptize me again, to fill me anew with the Holy Spirit. I don't want the best I can do; I want the best He can do. I want to remain in the right spiritual position all day, every day, prepared for what He has for me.

Throughout the day, pray in tongues. Practice and press in to this gift. I do it when I'm by myself, when I'm with my family, when I'm in the car, and when I'm in the shower. When I need help, I pray in tongues. When I need comfort, I pray in tongues. When I don't know what to pray for, I pray in tongues! I speak those mysteries to God so He can manifest them in my life. The more you do this, the more natural it will feel. The more accustomed you will be to having the presence of God with you all the time. The Holy Spirit will influence you and work through you in ways you've never experienced before.

Your life will never be the same!

APPENDIX

COMMON OBJECTIONS TO SPEAKING IN TONGUES

Speaking in tongues remains controversial to some people—though it shouldn't be. Let's look briefly at some objections I often hear from well-meaning believers.

Speaking in tongues is disruptive and unnecessary.

The primary text about speaking in tongues is 1 Corinthians 12–14. Here, Paul lays out information concerning the gifts of the Spirit (chapter 12), the motivation of the Spirit (chapter 13), and the voice of the Spirit (chapter 14). He addresses a local church environment, which he describes as chaotic, partly because some people spoke in tongues without any interpretation, leaving others confused.

I addressed this in chapter 8, but let me state again that Paul was writing to the Corinthian church, not an individual. These three chapters deal primarily with corporate behavior. Of course, we can read and benefit from them as individuals, as with everything in the Bible. But Paul's immediate purpose was to teach a congregation about the proper operation of tongues and prophecy in a corporate meeting. While personal prayer languages were not helpful in a group setting, speaking in tongues with interpretation was and is very helpful, as is prophecy. He was giving the proper context for the exercise of these three different gifts, not saying one was good and another bad.

By the way, I'll restate here that you and I can speak in tongues in church as long as it either (a) is not disruptive, calling attention to itself, or (b) has an interpretation. God gives us each a personal prayer language to use and enjoy. Paul's purpose was to supply guardrails, boundaries, and a safe and helpful way for this gift to function. Remember, the Corinthian church was something of a madhouse, probably nothing like most churches today. There was weird stuff going on there on many levels; some church members were even sleeping with their stepparents! Paul was trying to bring basic order to every aspect of life for those in this fledgling congregation. It wasn't just about speaking in tongues.

It's always helpful to remind ourselves that squeezed in between his explanation of the gifts of the Spirit and the voice of the Spirit is the motivation of the Spirit, which is always love. (Have a look at the beautiful and well-known chapter 13 of 1 Corinthians, which is all about love.) We must do everything, including prophesying and speaking in tongues, because of love. God is love. Love motivates everything He does.

Paul concluded his teaching by affirming that he prayed in the Spirit and in the understanding. Both are needed; neither should be excluded from the Christian life, though in congregational settings, speaking in tongues should always have an interpretation or be kept quiet so it doesn't become the focus of attention.

Speaking in tongues passed away with the apostles.

This common argument against speaking in tongues has no biblical basis, though some teachers distort a couple of verses to justify their argument. It's important to say that even these anti-tongues teachers admit that nowhere does the Bible say speaking in tongues has passed away or should pass away. The best they can do is badly twist the meaning of the following passage:

> But whether there are prophecies, they will fail; whether there are tongues, they will cease; whether there is knowledge, it will vanish away. For we know in part and we prophesy in part. But when that which is perfect has come, then that which is in part will be done away.
>
> —1 Corinthians 13:8–10

In a flight of imagination, these teachers posit that the "perfect" thing to come is the Bible. This makes no sense and has no other support in the Bible itself. Most scholars rightly say that the "perfect" means when Jesus comes again to rule the earth, and our present, imperfect forms of knowledge and prophecy are no longer needed or sufficient.

Further, the Bible testifies that gift of tongues was active two decades after it was first given on the day of Pentecost in Jerusalem. In Acts 19 Paul arrived in Ephesus and found a group of men following the teachings of John the Baptist. Paul updated them on the gospel message, then baptized them in water and laid hands on them for the baptism with the Holy Spirit. It says: "And when Paul had laid hands on them, the Holy Spirit came upon them, and they spoke with tongues and prophesied" (Acts 19:6).

This was twenty years after the day of Pentecost! Why would God give tongues two decades after Pentecost, then stop giving it after that? What is the logic of giving it for a certain season? Is there anything else in the Bible—and, in particular, any other spiritual gift—that He did that with? The answer is no.

The gifts of the Spirit were given to remain permanently, just as the power and presence of the Holy Spirit remain in us.

If I am baptized in the Holy Spirit, the Holy Spirit might take over my will and make me act strange.

Some people fear that if they come under the influence of the Holy Spirit and begin speaking in tongues, they will launch into some out-of-control state and look and feel ridiculous. Even though movies and documentaries depict spiritual experiences as ecstatic and chaotic, that is not how the Holy Spirit works. Let me assure you, He always works in cooperation with your will.

Other religions promote tantric practices, the clearing of one's mind, and the yielding of oneself to unknown powers (sometimes described as the universe, spirit guides, angels, and so on). But God is not in the business of taking over our wills. A great truth about Christianity is that it dignifies what God created—including the human freedom to choose. God never removes our prerogative to choose. He even lets people choose really bad things and make really bad choices about their lives, which is why the world is so full of evil.

Indeed, it is the enemy of our souls who tries to dominate our will and take control of our lives by force, intimidation, persuasion, and threat. That is not God's way and never has been. The entire Christian walk is about choosing Him (or not) every step of the way.

When we receive the baptism with the Holy Spirit, He will not override our wills and make us do what we don't want to. We always have a choice to yield to Him or not. Paul talks about tongues and other spiritual gifts happening as the Spirit wills. This means He expresses His will, and you choose to say yes or no. If you say yes to His will, your will unites with His, and the results are powerful.

This is nothing unusual for a Christian. We already do this when we pray, worship, obey, and so on. Speaking in tongues works the same way as all the spiritual practices we are familiar with. Paul wrote, "The spirits of the prophets are subject to the prophets" (1 Cor. 14:32). This means, in modern terms, that no one can say the Holy Spirit took over their mind and body and made them start prophesying or acting weird in the middle of the store or during a church service. We always have the option to choose.

That image of the Holy Spirit coming upon you and making you roll around in the aisle at the grocery store, speaking in unknown tongues, will not happen. It would impress nobody, and it's just not how God interacts with us. Some of us have experienced churches where people act like God took them over and made them do crazy things. The truth is, those people had a will every second of the way, and they can't rightfully blame it on God. They get to take full credit for what they did.

I like to describe the human will as the handle on a faucet. Much like the faucets in the story I shared in the introduction to this book, when connected to the right power source (the Holy Spirit), the faucets control the flow of that power in our lives. We turn on that flow through prayer, worship, Bible reading, speaking in tongues, prophesying, giving words of wisdom, and every other spiritual function. The Spirit of God becomes evident in our lives when we add our yeses to His yes. He is not out to control us; He is out to partner with us in willing cooperation.

Speaking in tongues is such an unknown, mysterious thing, and I want to understand it more fully before I say yes.

Most aspects of the Christian life start as mysteries. We are limited creatures. We are not all-knowing like God. But people who insist on understanding everything before yielding and participating will stay stuck at a low level of maturity forever. They don't grasp how mystery calls us up to greater levels of understanding.

Some Christians misunderstand the way the Bible uses the word *mysteries*. In everyday usage, a mystery is something we aren't meant to understand; it's something deliberately kept hidden. But in the Bible, mysteries are exactly the opposite: they are things we don't understand until we engage with them, trusting God in faith, at which point He releases knowledge and understanding equal to our faith. Mysteries, in the biblical sense, are meant to be revelations! That's how God works.

In the Book of Isaiah, God said, "'For My thoughts are not your thoughts, nor are your ways My ways,' says the LORD. 'For as the heavens are higher than the earth, so are My ways higher than your ways, and My thoughts than your thoughts'" (Isa. 55:8–9).

I have heard some teach that this verse means God's ways are so much higher than ours that there are some things we will never know. It's no good to try to solve God's mysteries. But if we look at the verses just before this one, we see it means exactly the opposite: "Seek the Lord while He may be found, call upon Him while He is near. Let the wicked forsake his way, and the unrighteous man his thoughts; let him return to the Lord, and He will have mercy on him; and to our God, for He will abundantly pardon" (vv. 6–7).

God's statement that His ways are higher than ours is His invitation to seek and understand His ways by faith. It's a promise that we can aspire to understand His mysteries by going after them! The Bible says we cannot please God without faith, and faith means moving forward and acting without full assurance or understanding. Walking with God always includes some level of unknown.

Job was a great example of this. He went through terrible suffering without understanding, yet he trusted God. Faith says, "I don't need to know; I just need to trust God."

As I walk with the Lord, I am more and more aware of what I don't know, rather than what I do know. This is the nature of our relationship with Christ, and we can't be afraid of that. To demand understanding before acting is actually a desire to control. If you understood everything you wanted to understand, you would be God!

Don't let a God complex keep you from pressing into

mysteries. Understanding will come as you welcome the influence of the Holy Spirit and say yes to whatever He has for you.

NOTES

Chapter 2

1. *Paraklesis* (παράκλησις, 3874) means "a calling to one's side" (*para*, "beside," *kaleo*, "to call"); W. E. Vine, Merrill F. Unger, and William White Jr., *Vine's Complete Expository Dictionary of Old and New Testament Words* (Nashville, TN: Thomas Nelson, 1996), 110.

Chapter 3

2. *Merriam-Webster*, s.v. "baptism," accessed April 4, 2023, https://www.merriam-webster.com/dictionary/baptism.

Printed in the USA
CPSIA information can be obtained
at www.ICGtesting.com
LVHW010603240424
778232LV00020B/1036